FOR ORGANS, PIANOS & ELECTRONIC KEYBOARDS

E-Z PLAY TODAY
102

The Christmas

2nd Edition

ISBN-13: 978-0-7935-0157-1

HAL•LEONARD®
CORPORATION

7777 W. BLUEMOUND RD. P.O. BOX 13819 MILWAUKEE, WI 53213

In Australia Contact:
Hal Leonard Australia Pty. Ltd.
4 Lentara Court
Cheltenham, Victoria, 3192 Australia
Email: ausadmin@halleonard.com

Angels We Have Heard on High

Registration 3
Rhythm: None

Traditional French Carol
Translated by James Chadwick

An - gels we have heard on high,
Shep - herds, we why have this heard ju - bi - lee?

sweet - ly sing - ing o'er the plains,
Why your joy - ous strains pro - long?
And the moun - tains
Say what may the

in re - ply ech - o - ing their joy - ous strains.
tid - ings be which in - spire your heaven - ly song?

Glo -

3

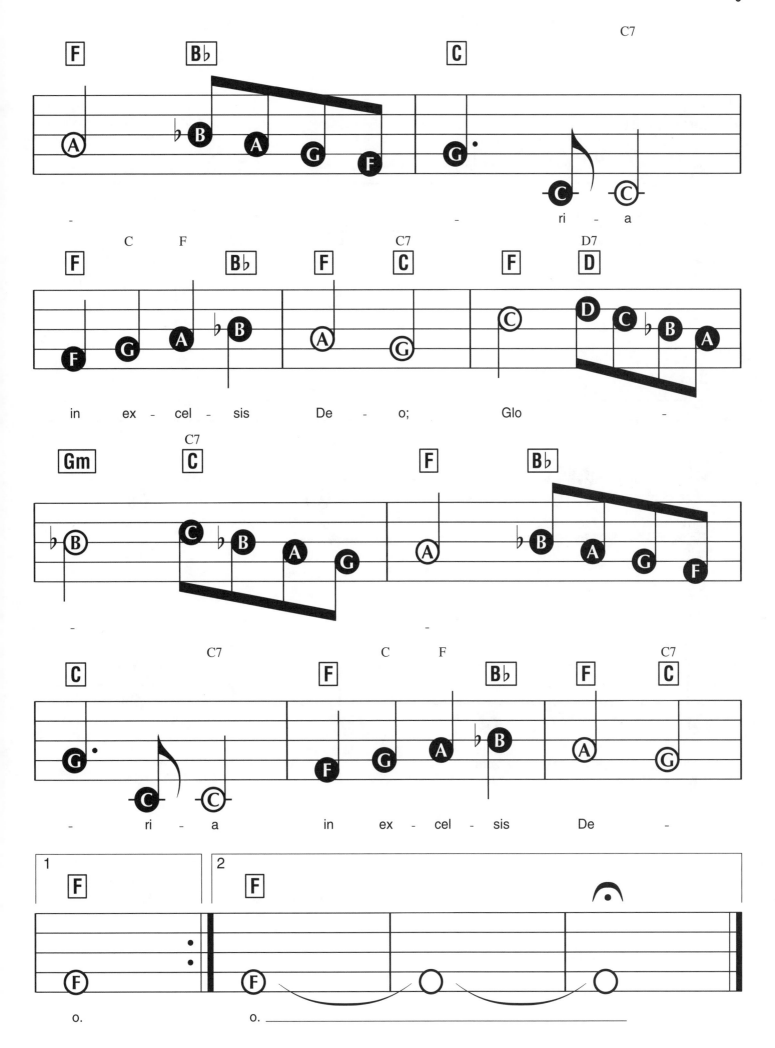

Away in a Manger

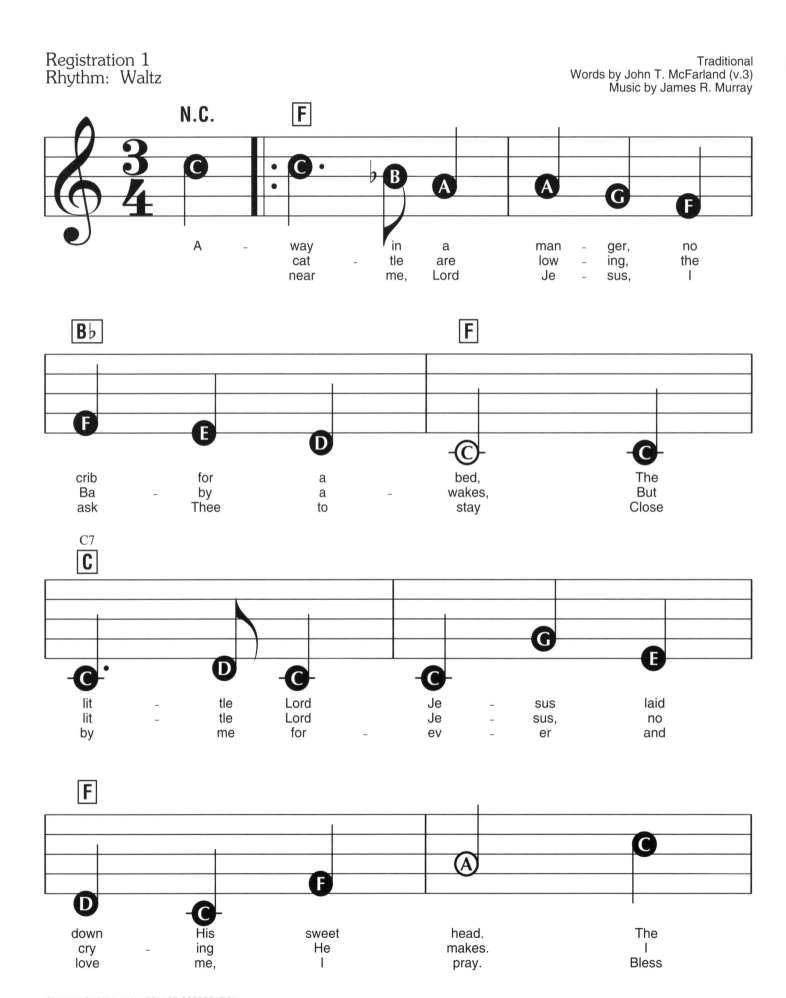

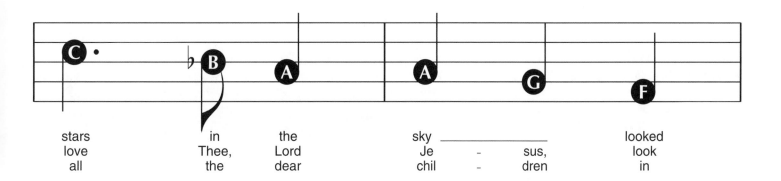

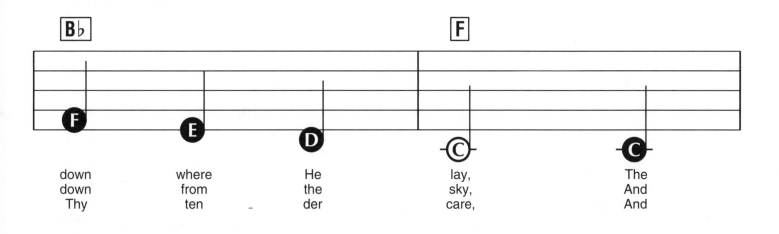

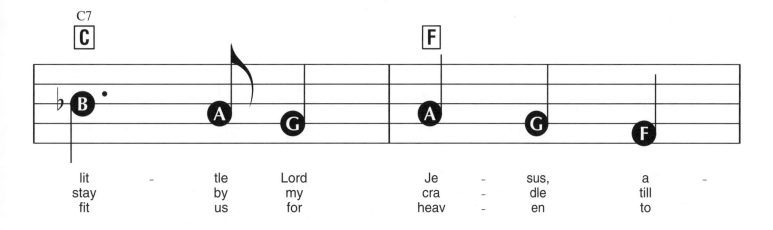

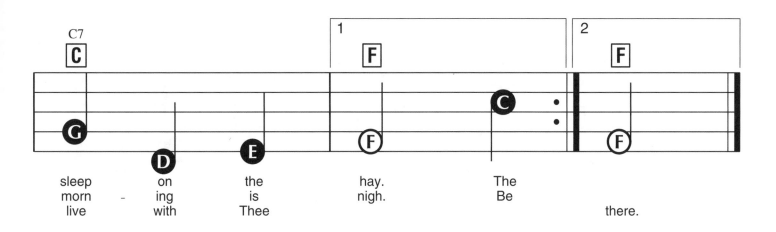

Christ Was Born on Christmas Day

Registration 6
Rhythm: None

Traditional

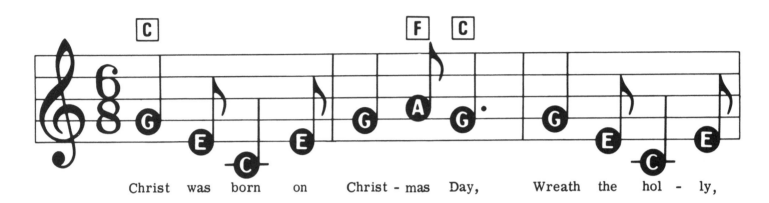

Christ was born on Christ - mas Day, Wreath the hol - ly,

twine the bay; Christ - us na - tus ho - di - e; The

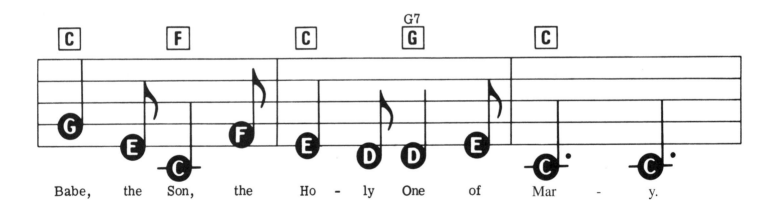

Babe, the Son, the Ho - ly One of Mar - y.

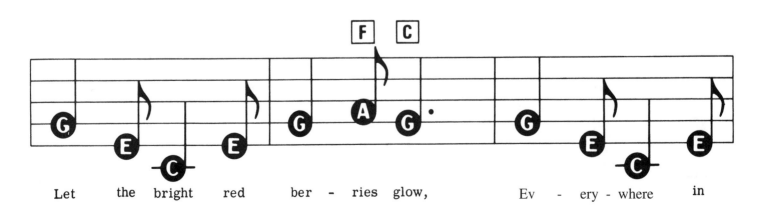

Let the bright red ber - ries glow, Ev - ery - where in

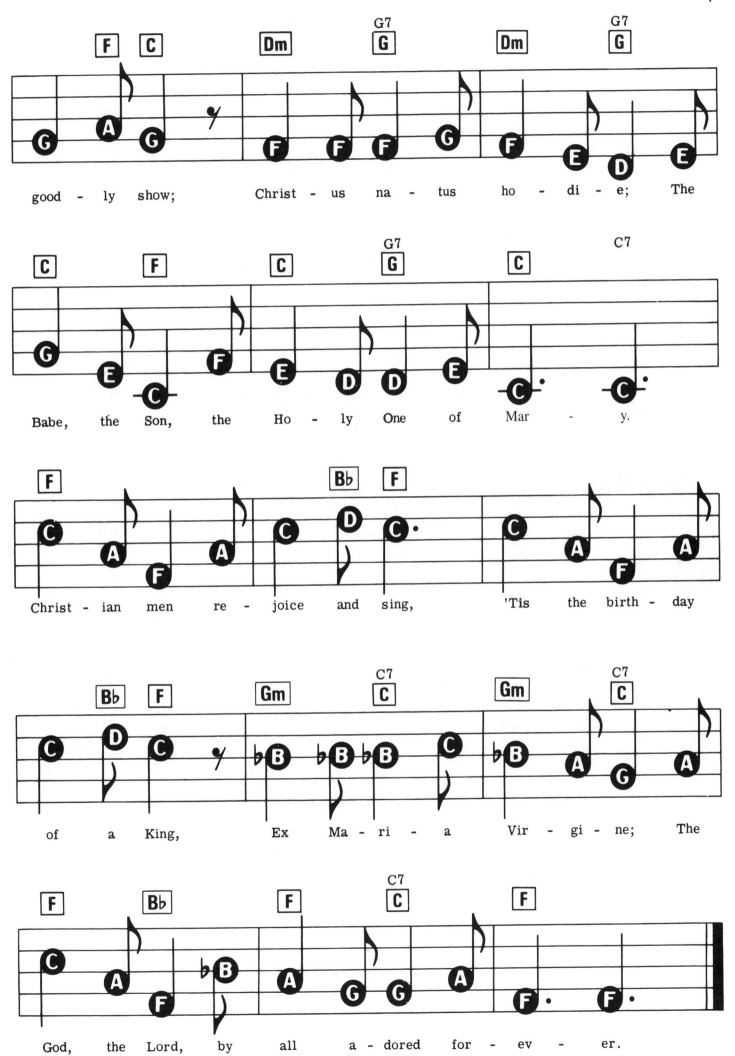

Deck the Hall

Registration 5
Rhythm: Fox Trot

Traditional Welsh Carol

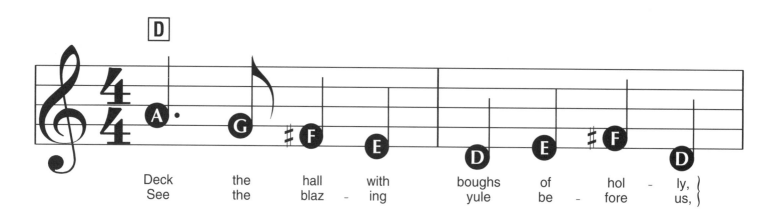

Deck the hall with boughs of hol - ly,
See the blaz - ing yule be - fore us,

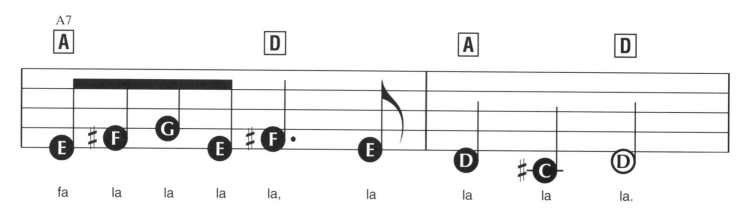

fa la la la la, la la la la.

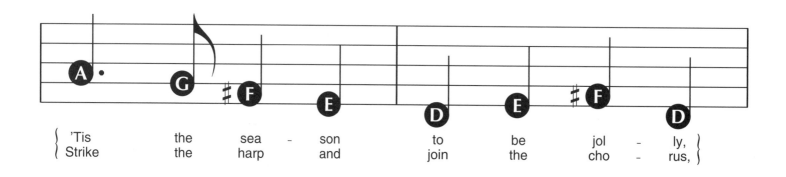

'Tis the sea - son to be jol - ly,
Strike the harp and join the cho - rus,

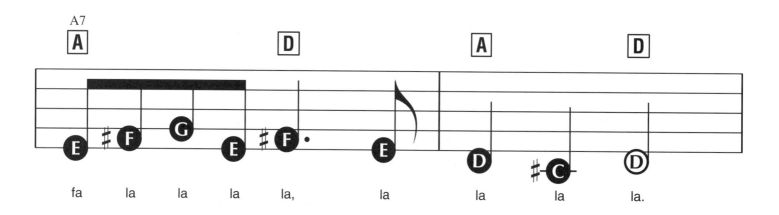

fa la la la la, la la la la.

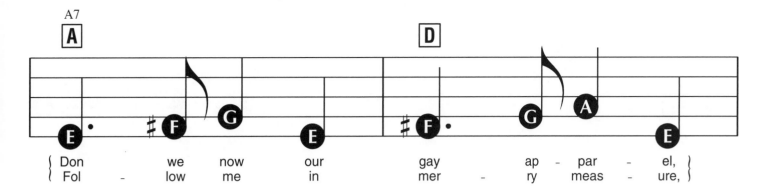

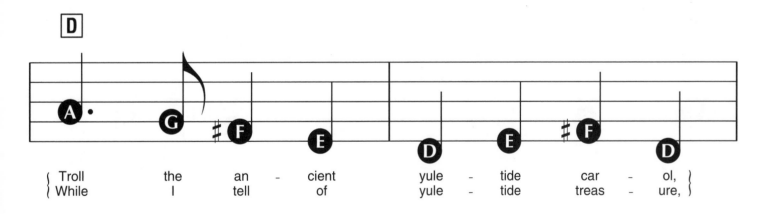

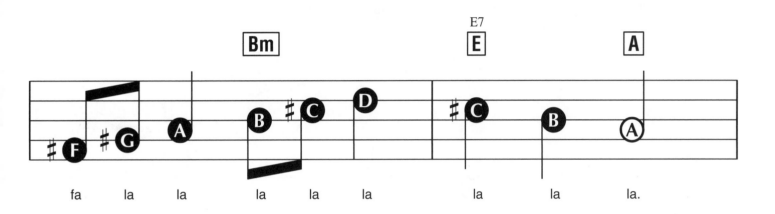

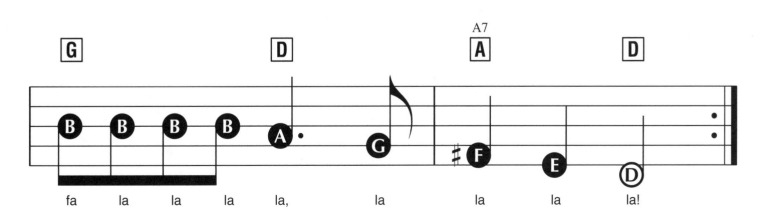

The First Noël

Registration 10
Rhythm: None

17th Century English Carol
Music from W. Sandys' *Christmas Carols*

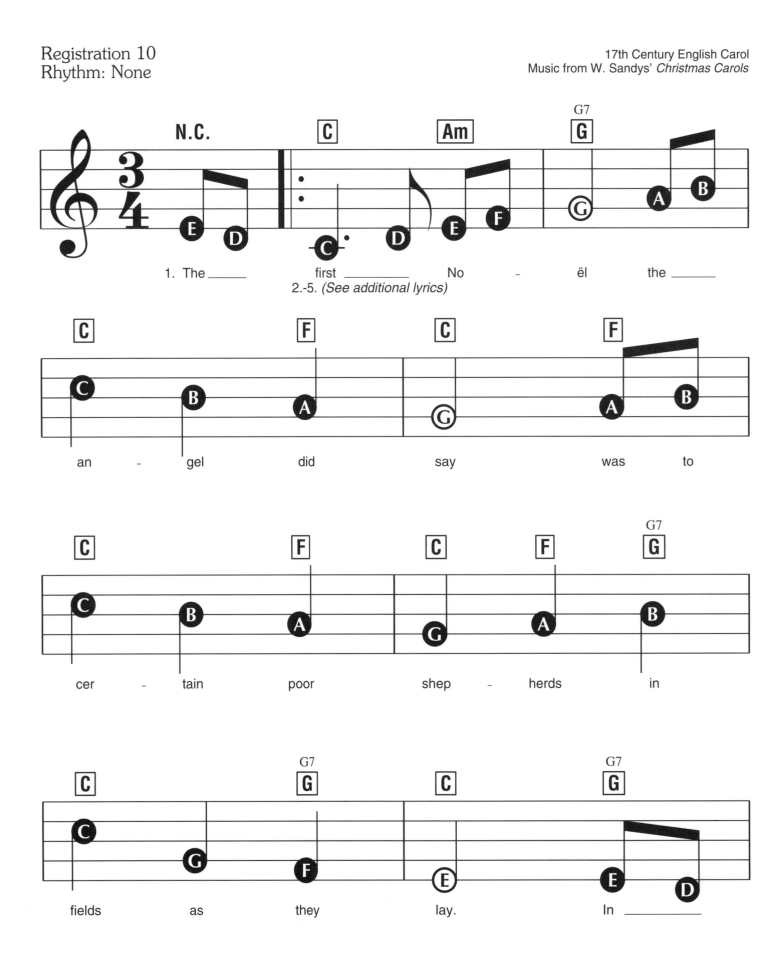

1. The ____ first _____ No - ël the ____
2.-5. *(See additional lyrics)*

an - gel did say was to

cer - tain poor shep - herds in

fields as they lay. In ____

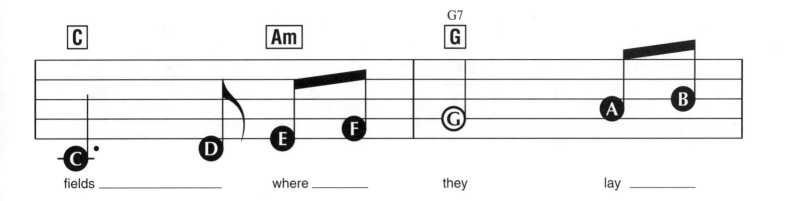

fields _____ where _____ they lay _____

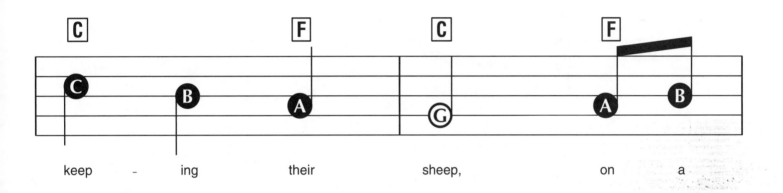

keep - ing their sheep, on a

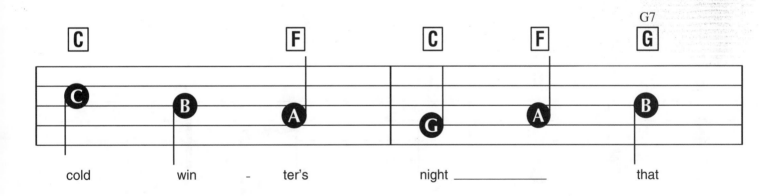

cold win - ter's night _____ that

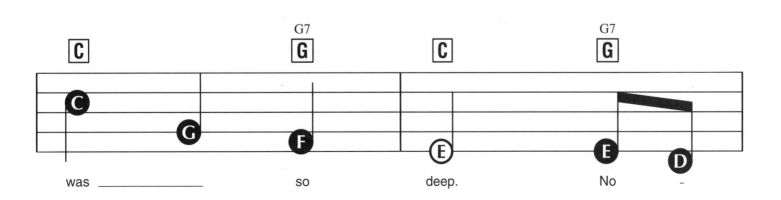

was _____ so deep. No -

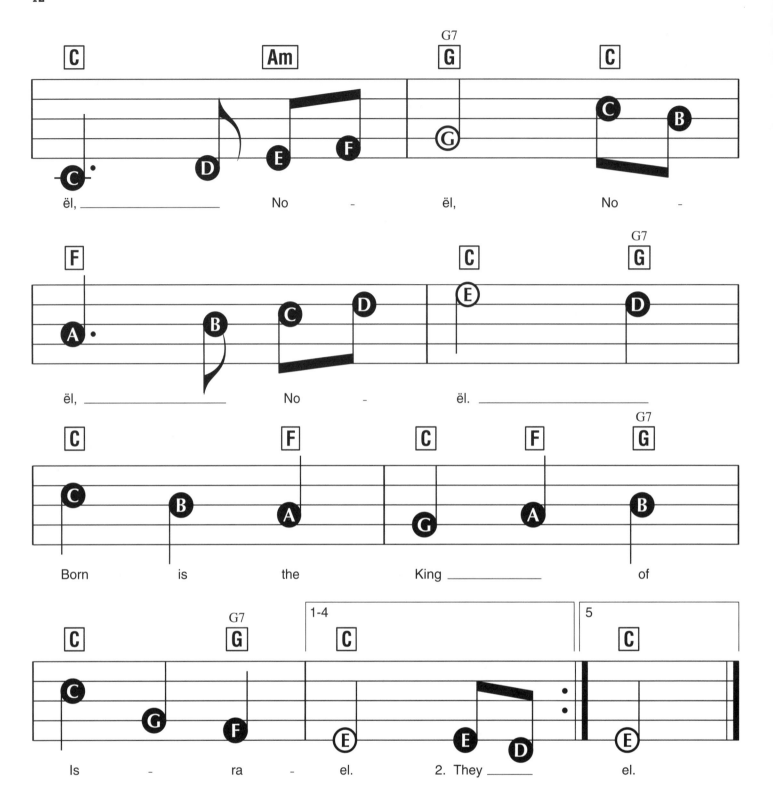

Additional Lyrics

2. They looked up and saw a star
   Shining in the east beyond them far.
   And to the earth it gave great light,
   And so it continued both day and night.
   Noël, Noël, Noël, Noël.
   Born is the King of Israel.

3. And by the light of that same star
   Three wise men came from country far.
   To seek for a King was their intent,
   And to follow the star wherever it went.
   Noël, Noël, Noël, Noël.
   Born is the King of Israel.

4. This star drew nigh to the northwest,
   O'er Bethlehem it took its rest.
   And there it did both stop and stay
   Right over the place where Jesus lay.
   Noël, Noël, Noël, Noël.
   Born is the King of Israel.

5. Then entered in those wise men three
   Full reverently upon their knee.
   And offered there, in His presence,
   Their gold, and myrrh, and frankincense.
   Noël, Noël, Noël, Noël.
   Born is the King of Israel.

Go, Tell It on the Mountain

Registration 5
Rhythm: Swing

African-American Spiritual
Verses by John W. Work, Jr.

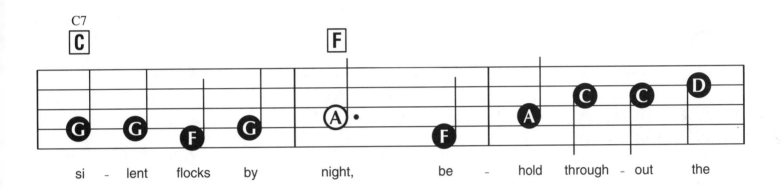

While shep - herds kept their watch - ing o'er

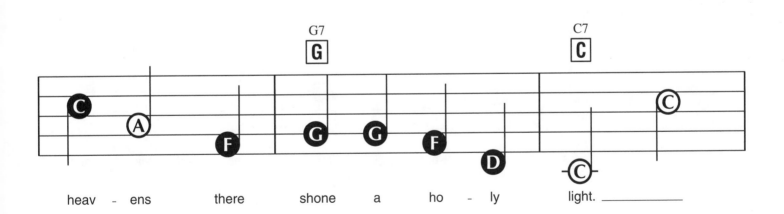

si - lent flocks by night, be - hold through - out the

heav - ens there shone a ho - ly light. ____

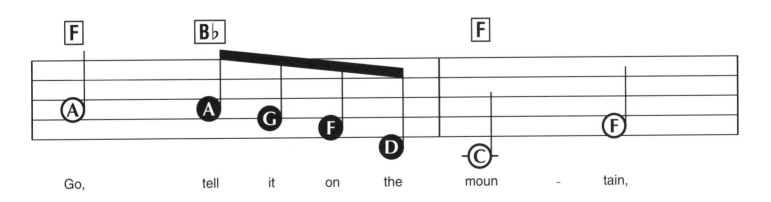

Go, tell it on the moun - tain,

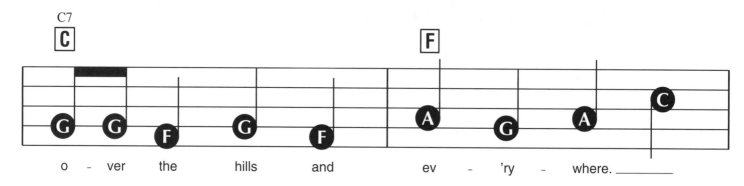

o - ver the hills and ev - 'ry - where. _____

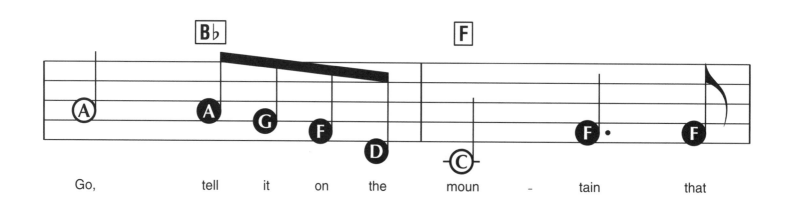

Go, tell it on the moun - tain that

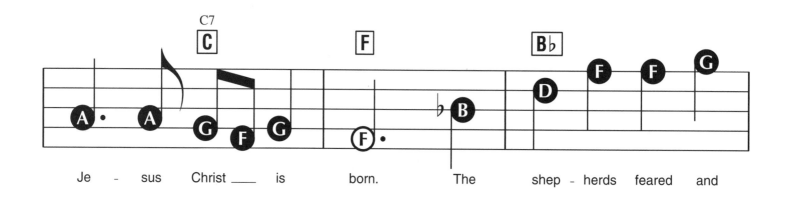

Je - sus Christ ___ is born. The shep - herds feared and

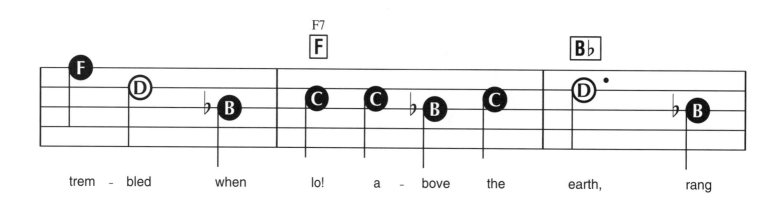

trem - bled when lo! a - bove the earth, rang

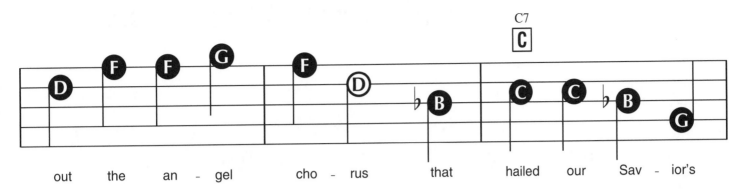

out the an - gel cho - rus that hailed our Sav - ior's

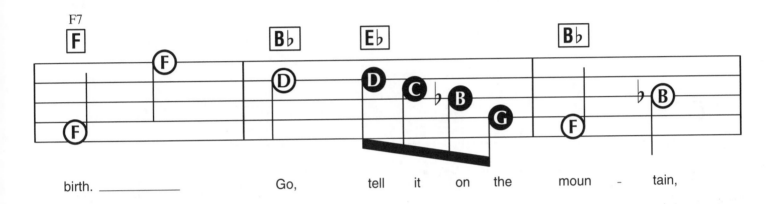

birth. _____ Go, tell it on the moun - tain,

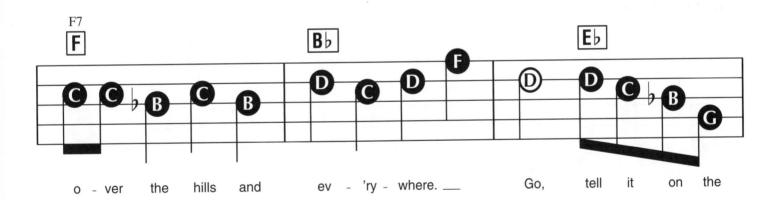

o - ver the hills and ev - 'ry - where. ___ Go, tell it on the

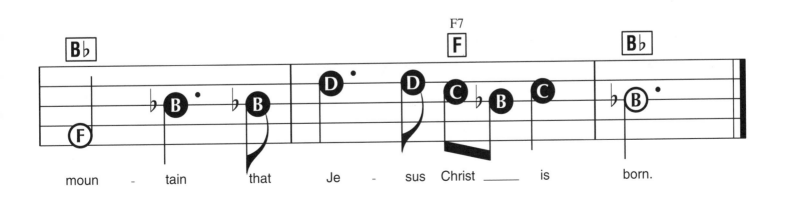

moun - tain that Je - sus Christ ___ is born.

God Rest Ye Merry, Gentlemen

Registration 6
Rhythm: None

19th Century English Carol

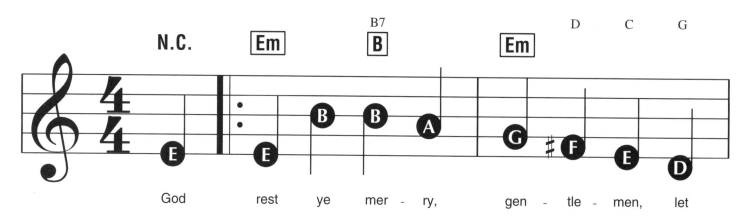

God rest ye mer - ry, gen - tle - men, let

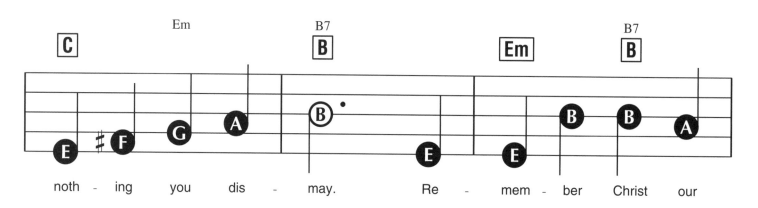

noth - ing you dis - may. Re - mem - ber Christ our

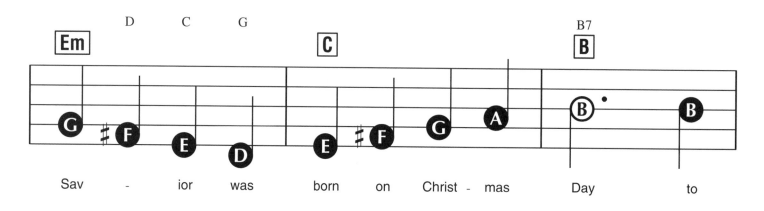

Sav - ior was born on Christ - mas Day to

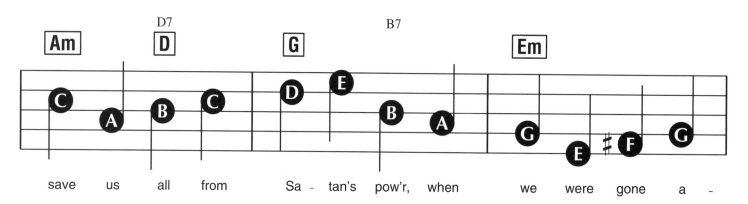

save us all from Sa - tan's pow'r, when we were gone a -

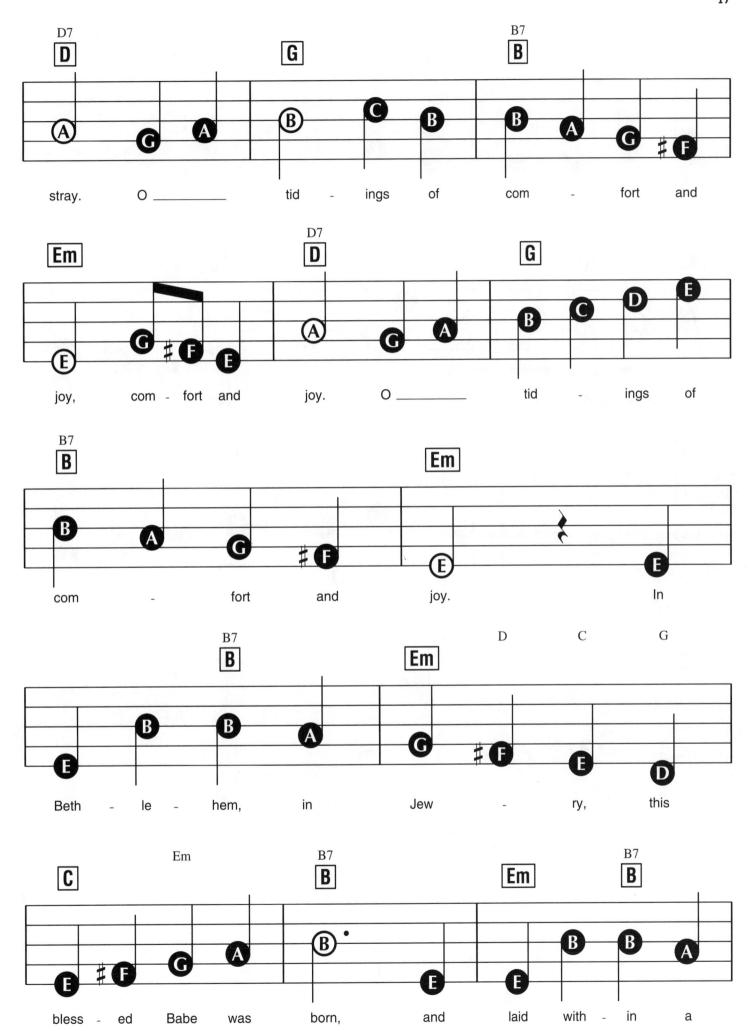

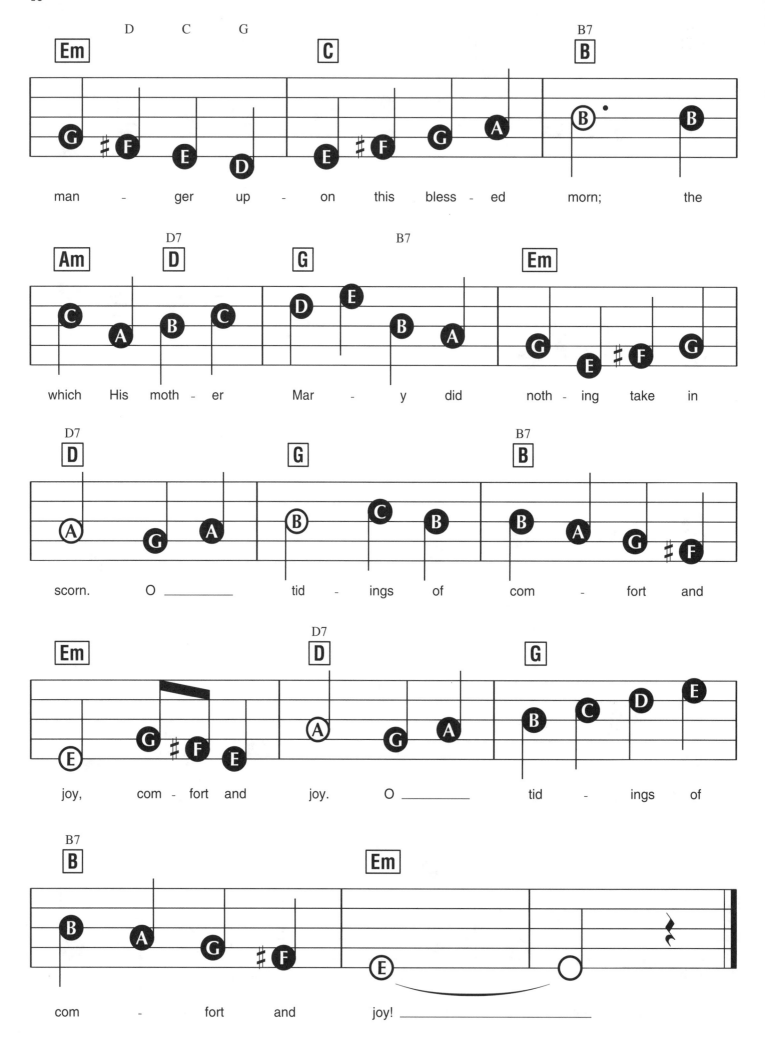

Good King Wenceslas

Registration 4
Rhythm: March

Words by John M. Neale
Music from *Piae Cantiones*

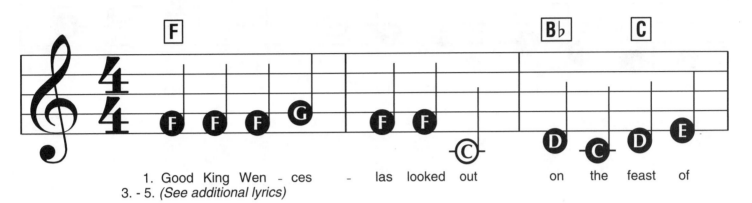

1. Good King Wen - ces - las looked out on the feast of
3. - 5. *(See additional lyrics)*

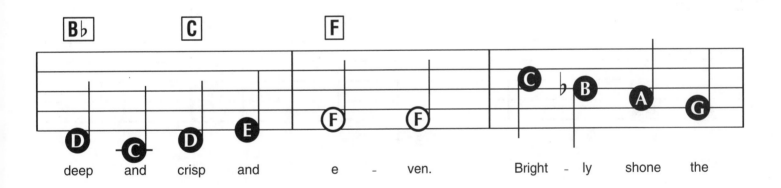

Ste - phen, when the snow lay 'round a - bout,

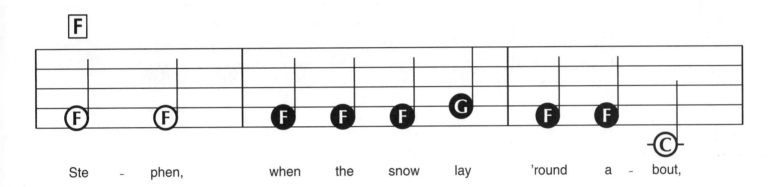

deep and crisp and e - ven. Bright - ly shone the

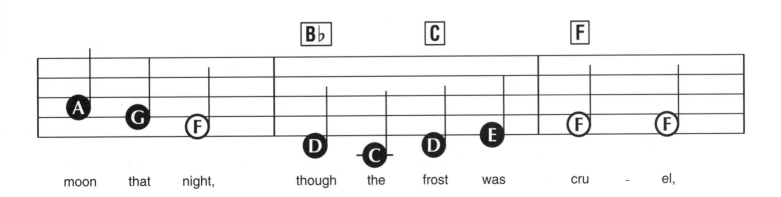

moon that night, though the frost was cru - el,

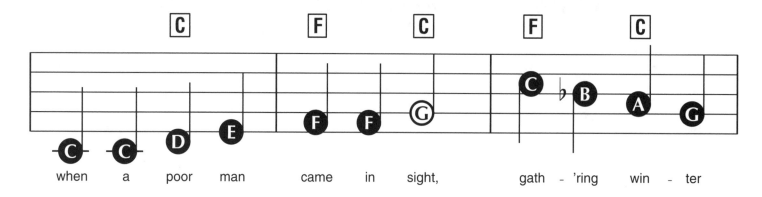

when a poor man came in sight, gath - 'ring win - ter

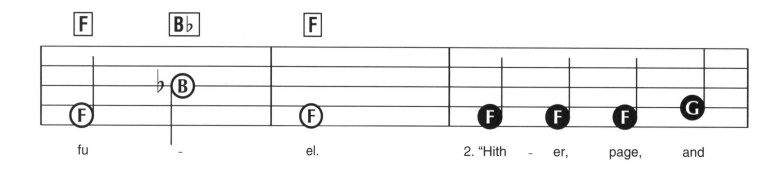

fu - el. 2. "Hith - er, page, and

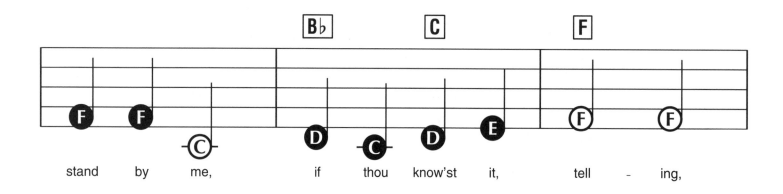

stand by me, if thou know'st it, tell - ing,

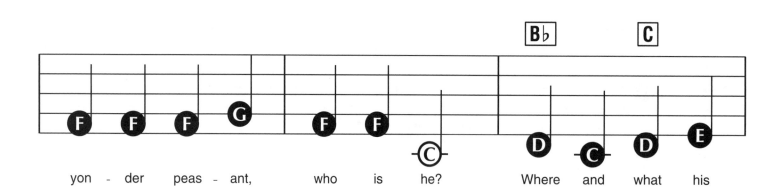

yon - der peas - ant, who is he? Where and what his

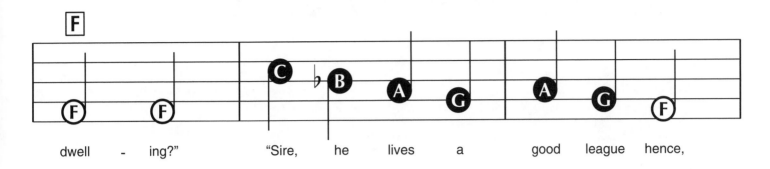

dwell - ing?" "Sire, he lives a good league hence,

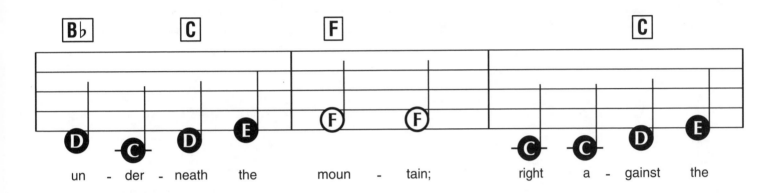

un - der - neath the moun - tain; right a - gainst the

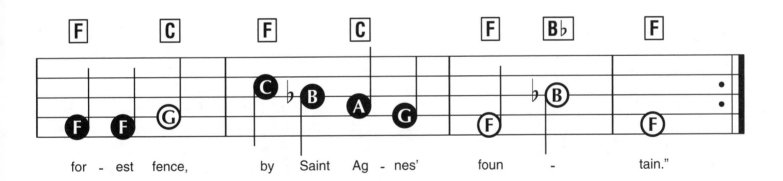

for - est fence, by Saint Ag - nes' foun - tain."

Additional Lyrics

3. "Bring me flesh, and bring me wine,
   Bring me pine logs hither.
   Thou and I will see him dine,
   When we bear them thither."
   Page and monarch forth they went,
   Forth they went together,
   Through the rude wind's wild lament
   And the bitter weather.

4. "Sire, the night is darker now,
   And the wind blows stronger.
   Fails my heart, I know not how,
   I can go no longer."
   "Mark my footsteps, my good page,
   Tread thou in them boldly.
   Thou shalt find the winter's rage
   Freeze thy blood less coldly."

5. In his master's steps he trod,
   Where the snow lay dinted;
   Heat was in the very sod
   Which the saint had printed.
   Therefore, Christian men, be sure,
   Wealth or rank possessing,
   Ye who now will bless the poor
   Shall yourselves find blessing.

Good Christian Men, Rejoice

Registration 6
Rhythm: None

14th Century Latin Text
Translated by John Mason Neale
14th Century German Melody

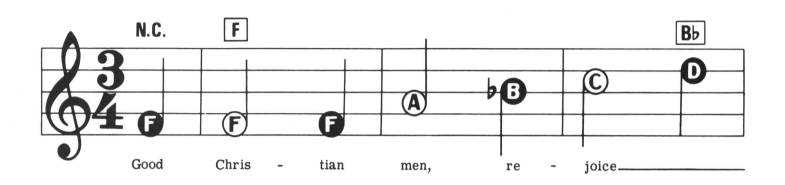

Good Chris - tian men, re - joice_____

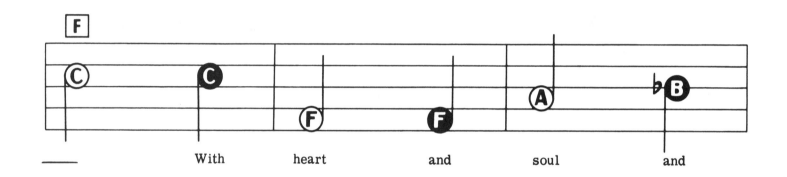

_____ With heart and soul and

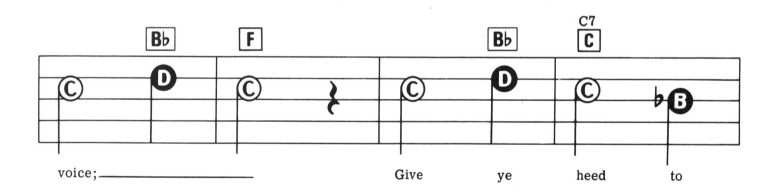

voice;_____ Give ye heed to

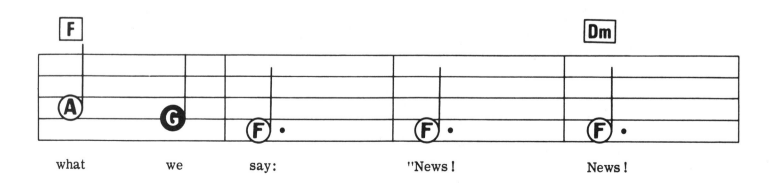

what we say: "News! News!

Hark! The Herald Angels Sing

Words by Charles Wesley
Altered by George Whitefield
Music by Felix Mendelssohn-Bartholdy
Arranged by William H. Cummings

Registration 5
Rhythm: None

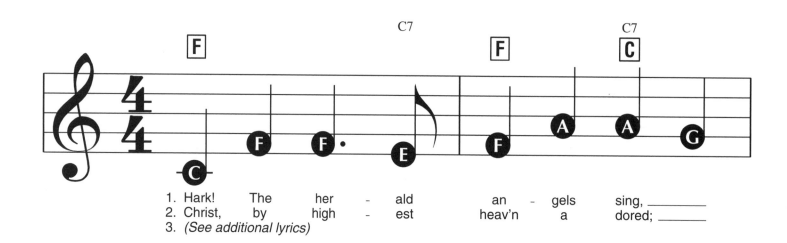

1. Hark! The her - ald an - gels sing, _____
2. Christ, by high - est heav'n a - dored; _____
3. *(See additional lyrics)*

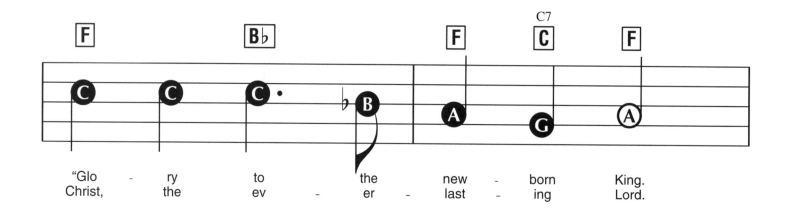

"Glo - ry to the new - born King.
Christ, the ev - er - last - ing Lord.

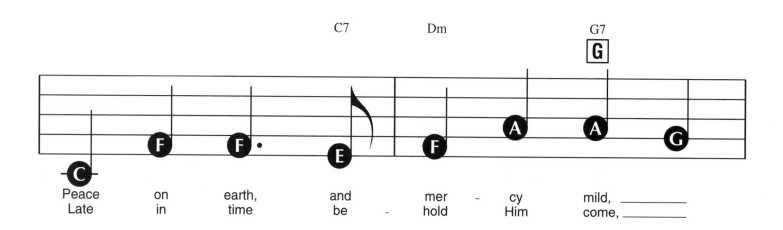

Peace on earth, and mer - cy mild, _____
Late in time be - hold Him come, _____

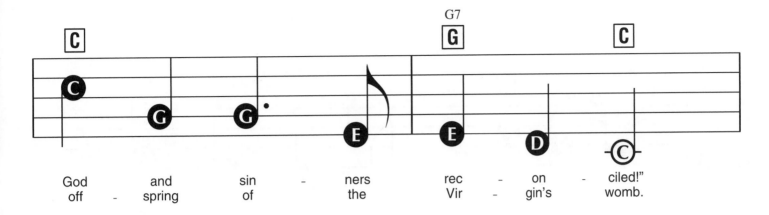

God   and   sin -   ners   rec -   on -   ciled!"
off -   spring   sin of   the   Vir -   gin's   womb.

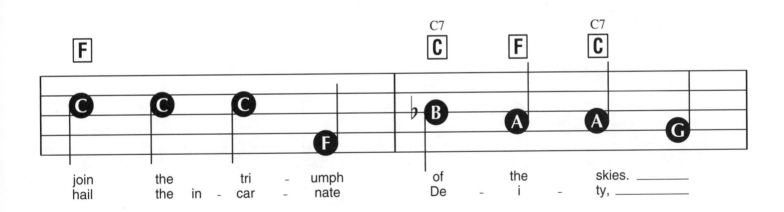

Joy -   ful,   all   ye   na -   tions.   rise, _____
Veiled   in   flesh   the   God -   head   see; _____

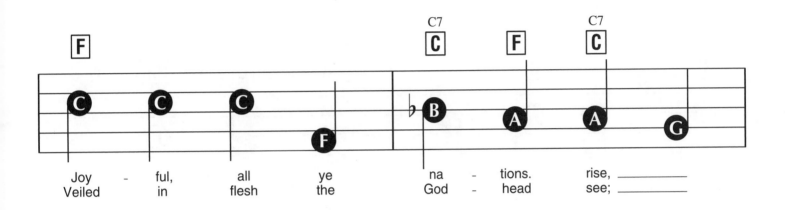

join   the   tri - umph   of   the   skies. _____
hail   the in - car - nate   De - i - ty, _____

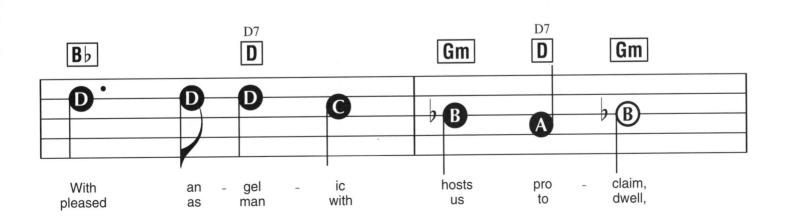

With   an - gel - ic   hosts   pro - claim,
pleased   as man   with   us   to   dwell,

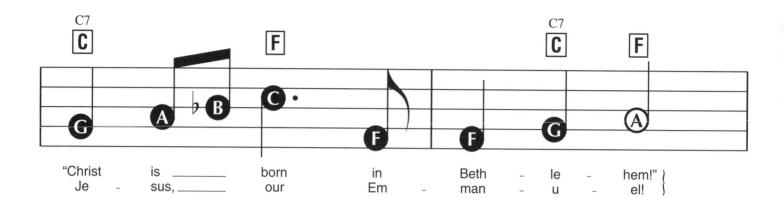

"Christ is _____ born in Beth - le - hem!"
Je - sus, _____ our Em - man - u - el!

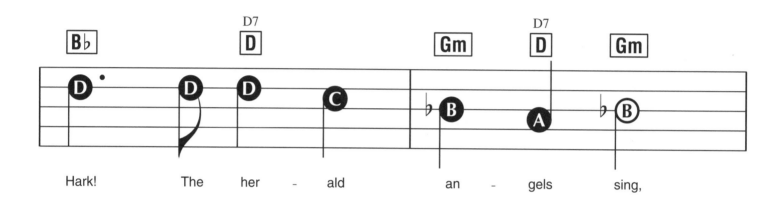

Hark! The her - ald an - gels sing,

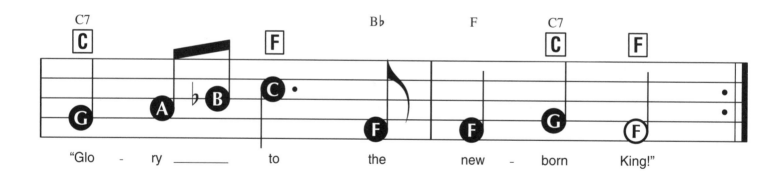

"Glo - ry _____ to the new - born King!"

Additional Lyrics

3. Hail the heaven-born Prince of Peace!
   Hail the sun of righteousness!
   Light and life to all he brings,
   Risen with healing in His wings.
   Mild He lays His glory by,
   Born that man no more may die.
   Born to raise the sons of earth,
   Born to give them second birth.

   Hark! The herald angels sing,
   "Glory to the newborn King!"

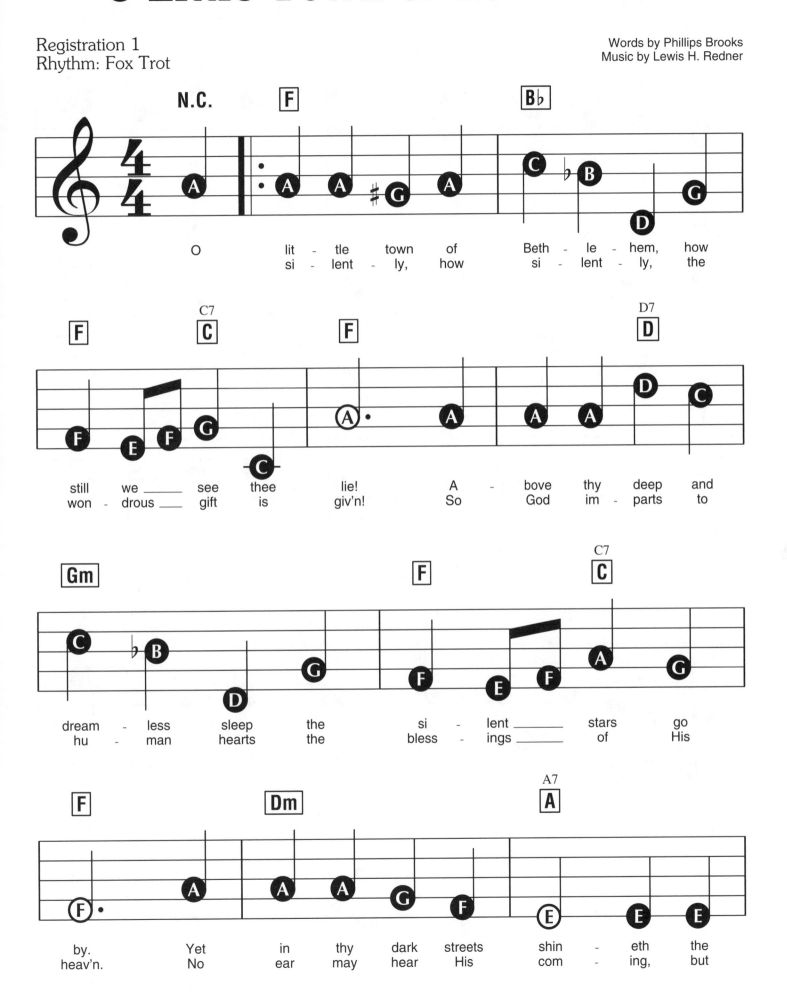

O Little Town of Bethlehem

Registration 1
Rhythm: Fox Trot

Words by Phillips Brooks
Music by Lewis H. Redner

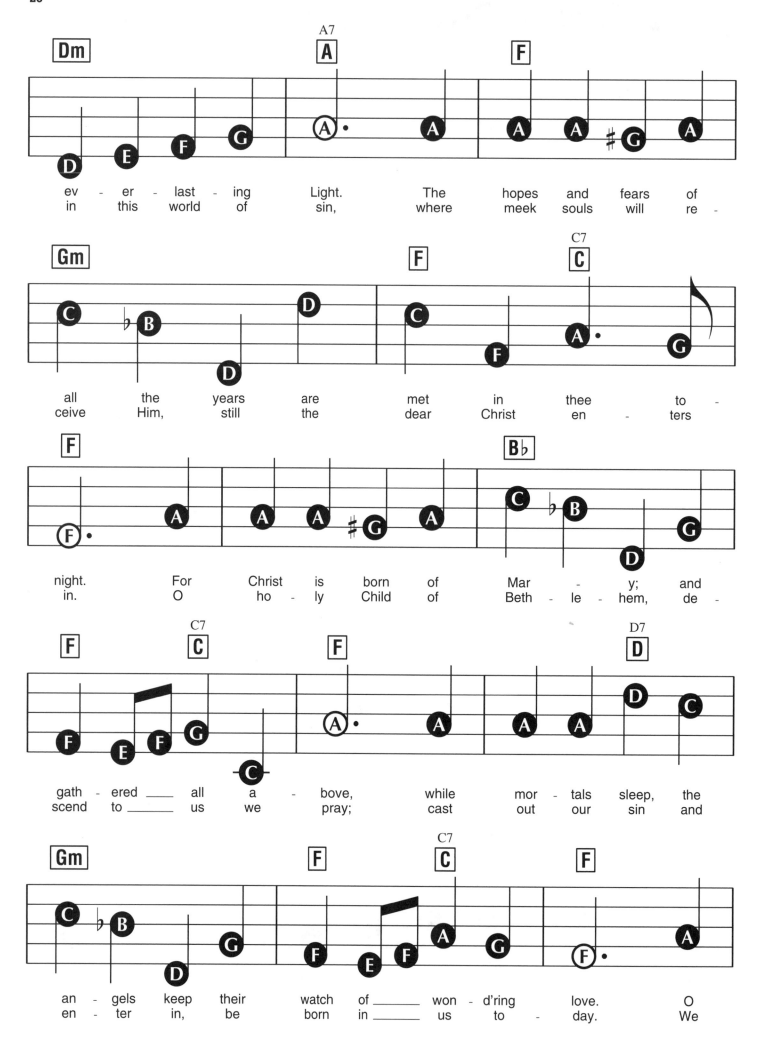

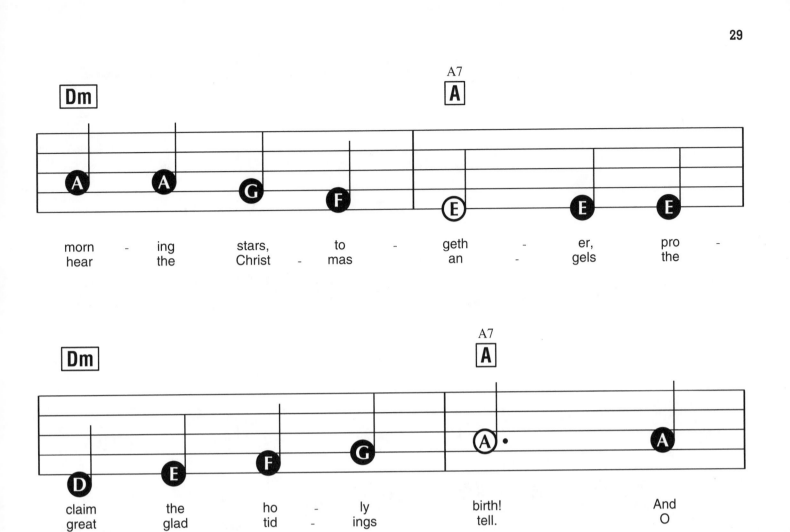

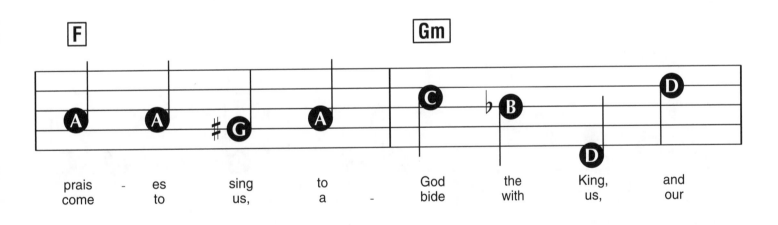

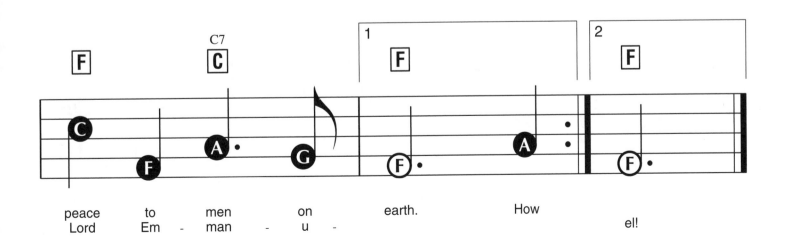

I Heard the Bells on Christmas Day

Registration 7
Rhythm: Ballad or Fox Trot

Words by Henry Wadsworth Longfellow
Music by John Baptiste Calkin

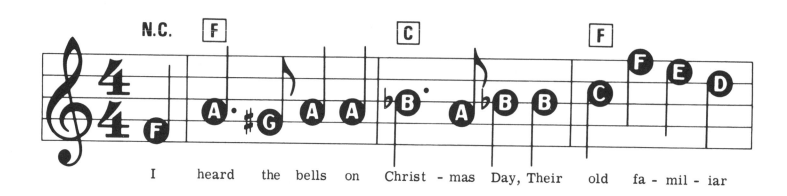

I heard the bells on Christ - mas Day, Their old fa - mil - iar

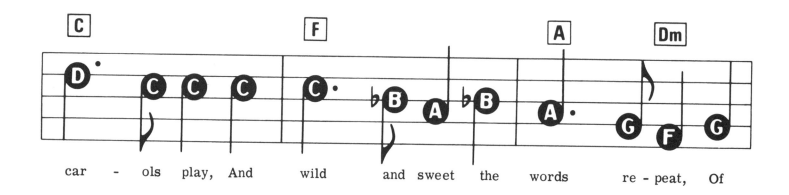

car - ols play, And wild and sweet the words re - peat, Of

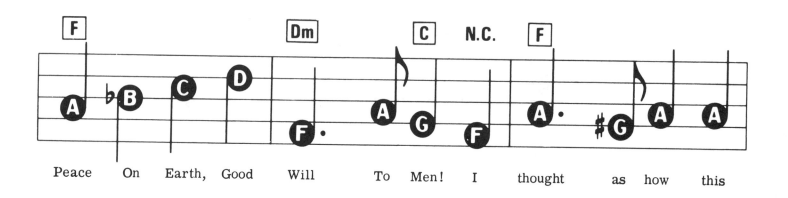

Peace On Earth, Good Will To Men! I thought as how this

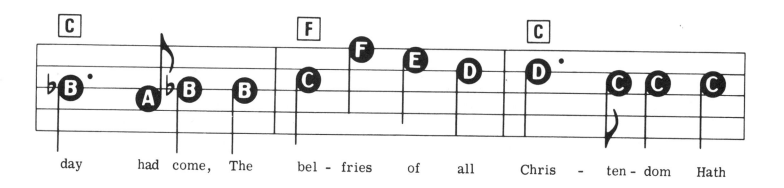

day had come, The bel - fries of all Chris - ten - dom Hath

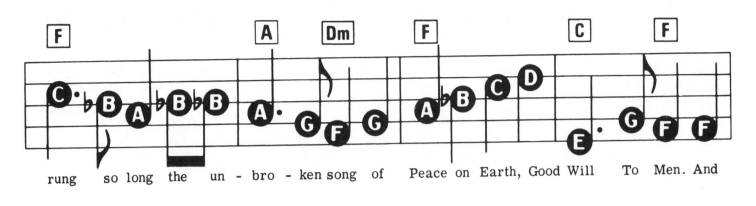

rung so long the un - bro - ken song of Peace on Earth, Good Will To Men. And

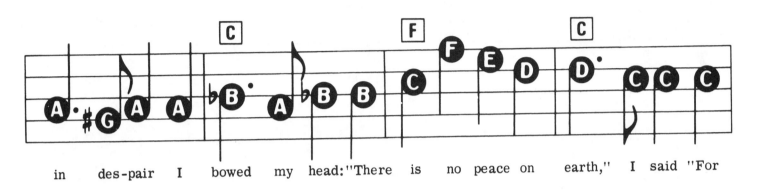

in des-pair I bowed my head: "There is no peace on earth," I said "For

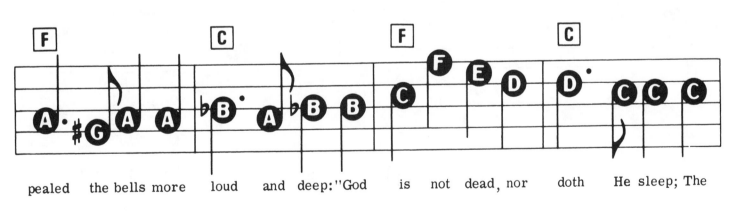

hate is strong and mocks the song of Peace On Earth, Good Will To Men." Then

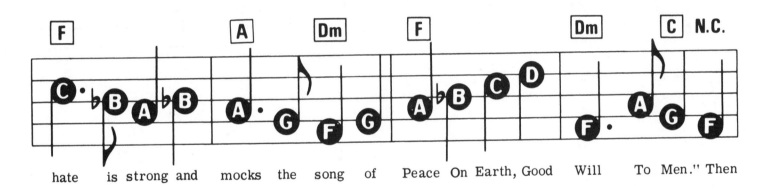

pealed the bells more loud and deep: "God is not dead, nor doth He sleep; The

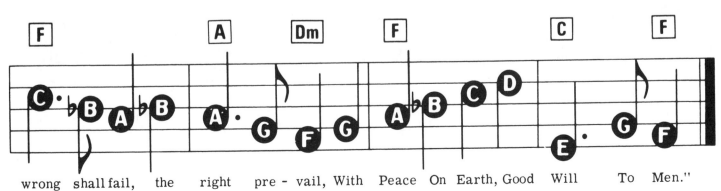

wrong shall fail, the right pre - vail, With Peace On Earth, Good Will To Men."

It Came Upon the Midnight Clear

Registration 1
Rhythm: None

Words by Edmund Hamilton Sears
Music by Richard Storrs Willis

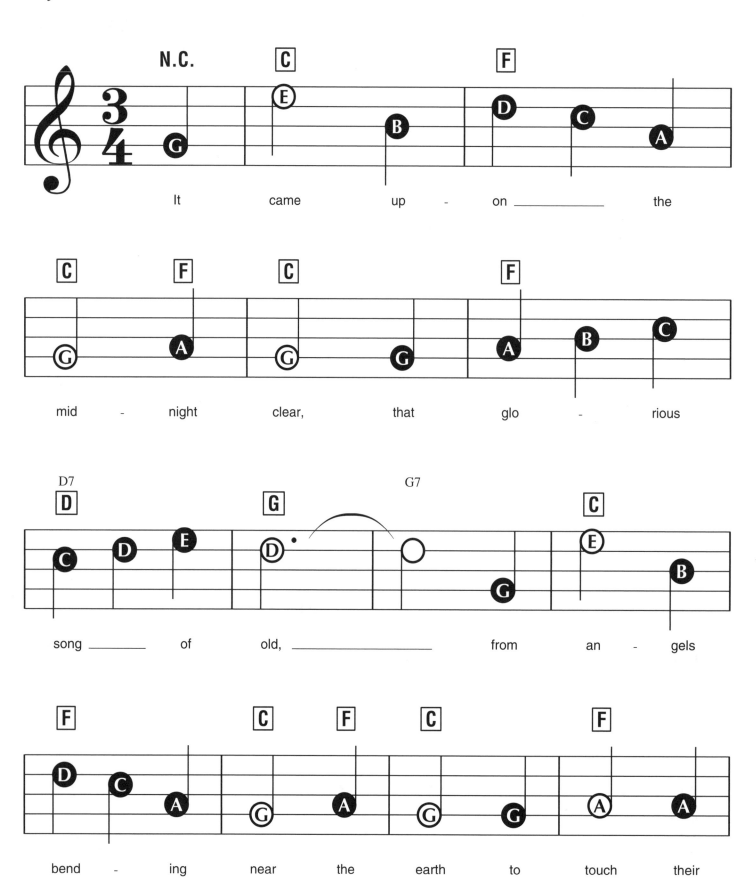

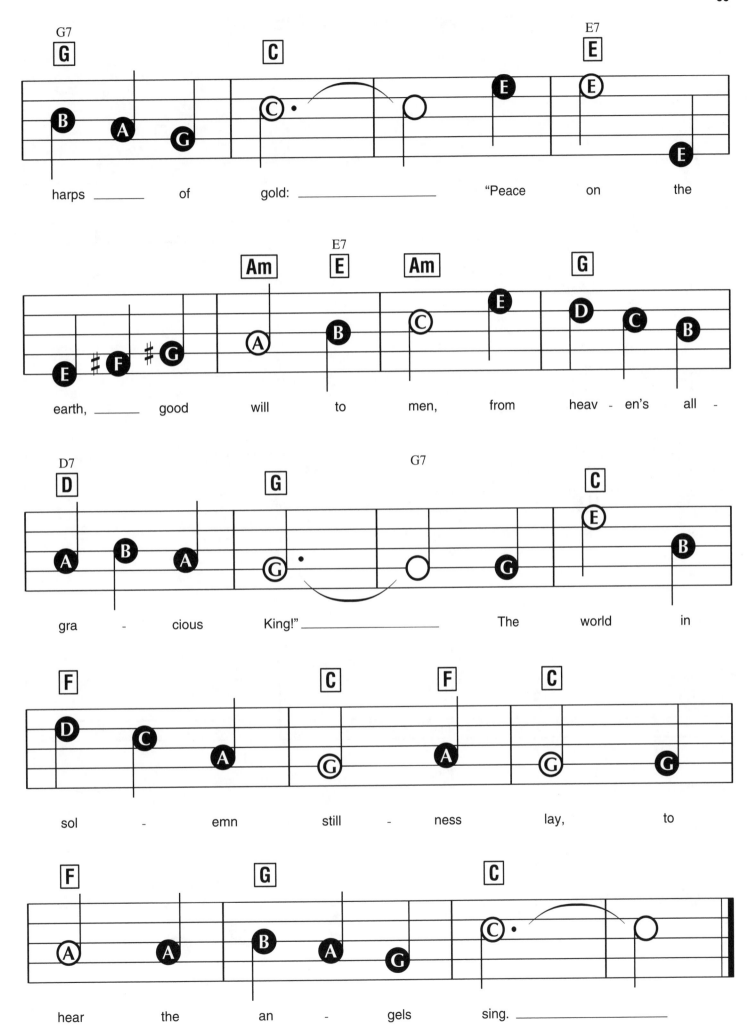

Joy to the World

Registration 2
Rhythm: None

Words by Isaac Watts
Music by George Frideric Handel
Arranged by Lowell Mason

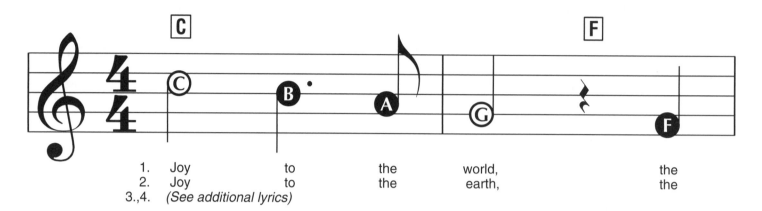

1. Joy to the world, the
2. Joy to the the earth, the
3.,4. *(See additional lyrics)*

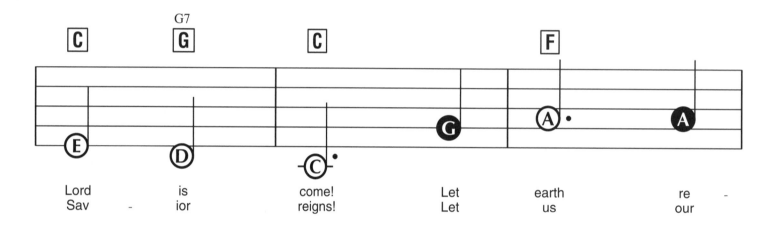

Lord is come! Let earth re -
Sav - ior reigns! Let us our

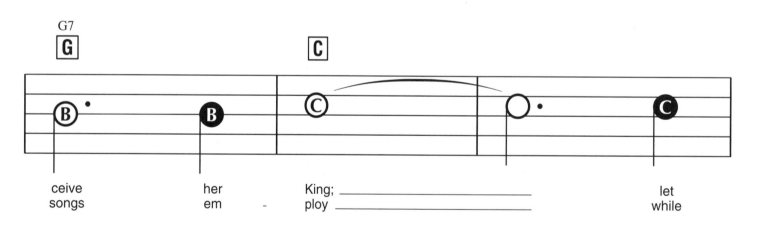

ceive her King; _____ let
songs her em - ploy _____ while

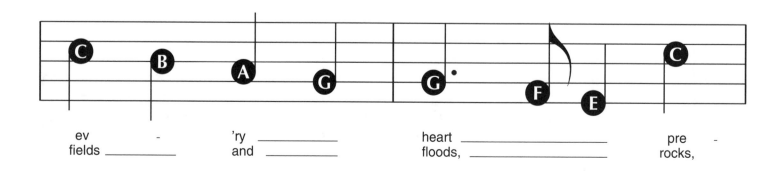

ev - 'ry _____ heart _____ pre -
fields _____ and _____ floods, _____ rocks,

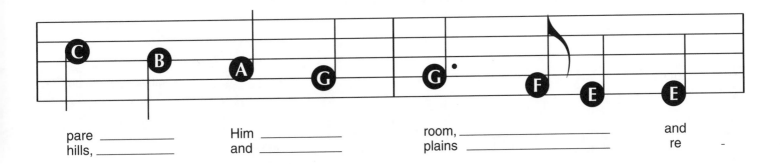

pare _____ Him _____ room, _____ and
hills, _____ and _____ plains _____ re -

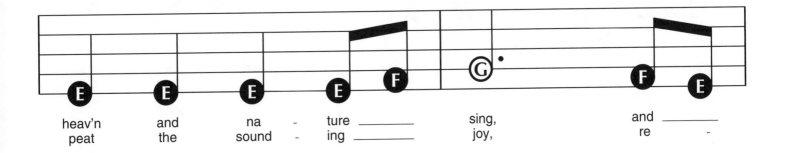

heav'n and na - ture _____ sing, and _____
peat and the sound - ing _____ joy, re -

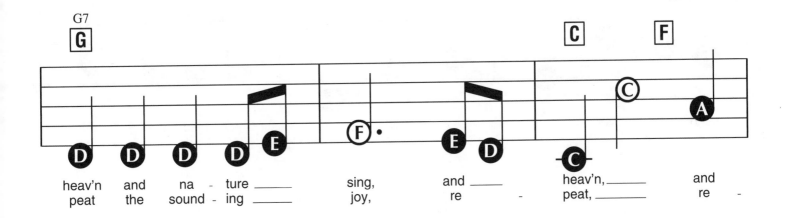

heav'n and na - ture _____ sing, and _____ heav'n, _____ and
peat the sound - ing _____ joy, and re - peat, _____ re -

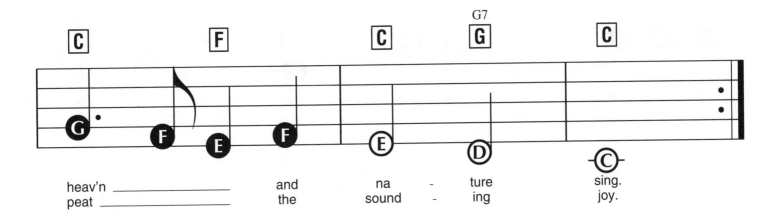

heav'n _____ and na - ture sing.
peat _____ the sound - ing joy.

Additional Lyrics

3. No more let sins and sorrows grow,
   Nor thorns infest the ground;
   He comes to make His blessings flow
   Far as the curse is found.

4. He rules the world with truth and grace,
   And makes the nations prove
   The glories of His righteousness
   And wonders of His love.

O Christmas Tree

Registration 3
Rhythm: None

Traditional German Carol

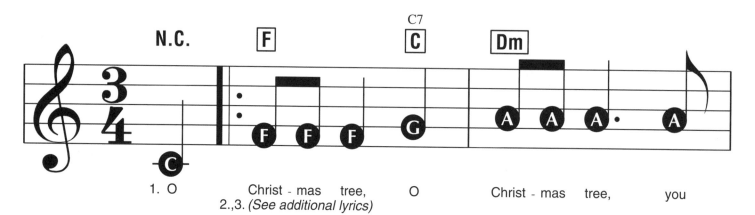

1. O Christ-mas tree, O Christ-mas tree, you
2.,3. *(See additional lyrics)*

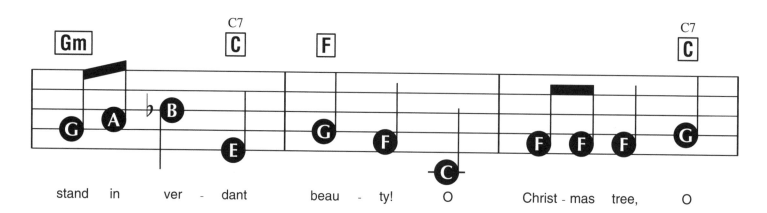

stand in ver-dant beau-ty! O Christ-mas tree, O

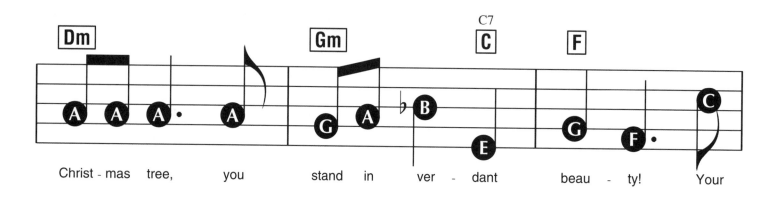

Christ-mas tree, you stand in ver-dant beau-ty! Your

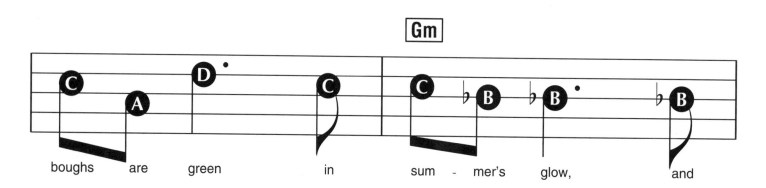

boughs are green in sum-mer's glow, and

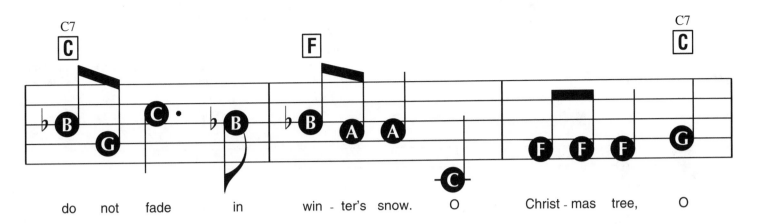

do not fade in win - ter's snow. O Christ - mas tree, O

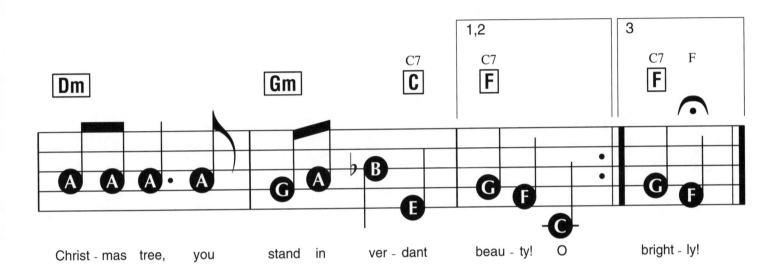

Christ - mas tree, you stand in ver - dant beau - ty! O bright - ly!

Additional Lyrics

2. O Christmas tree, O Christmas tree,
   Much pleasure dost thou bring me!
   O Christmas tree, O Christmas tree,
   Much pleasure dost thou bring me!
   For ev'ry year the Christmas tree
   Brings to us all both joy and glee.
   O Christmas tree, O Christmas tree,
   Much pleasure dost thou bring me!

3. O Christmas tree, O Christmas tree,
   Thy candles shine out brightly!
   O Christmas tree, O Christmas tree,
   Thy candles shine out brightly!
   Each bough doth hold its tiny light
   That makes each toy to sparkle bright.
   O Christmas tree, O Christmas tree,
   Thy candles shine out brightly!

O Come, All Ye Faithful
(Adeste fideles)

Registration 6
Rhythm: None

Words and Music by John Francis Wade
Latin Words translated by Frederick Oakeley

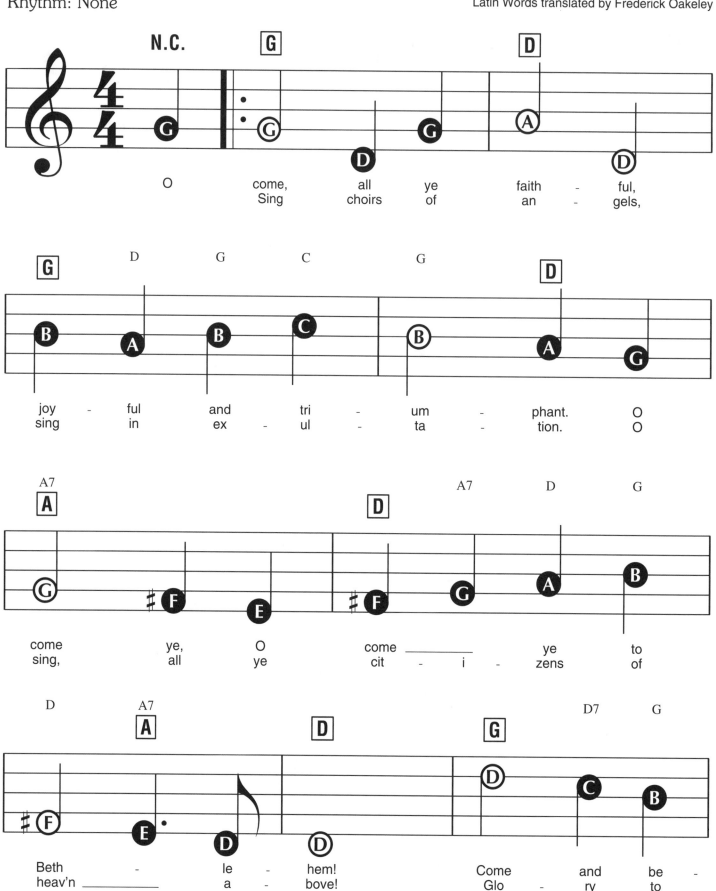

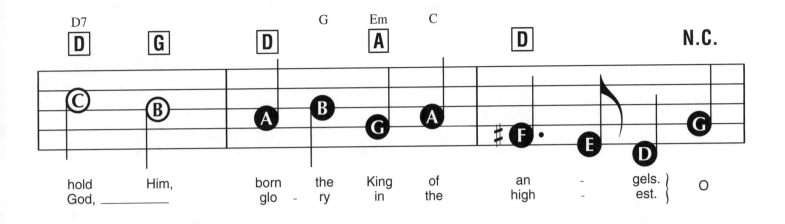

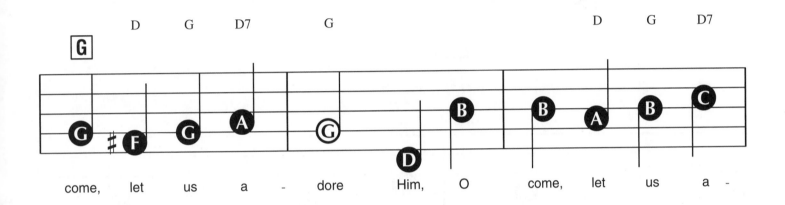

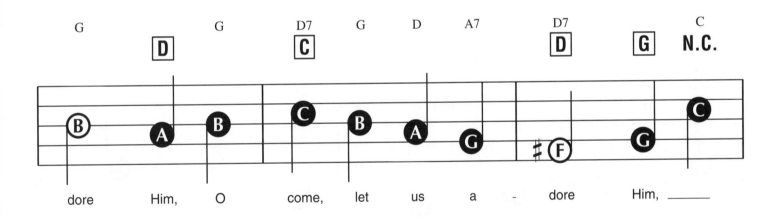

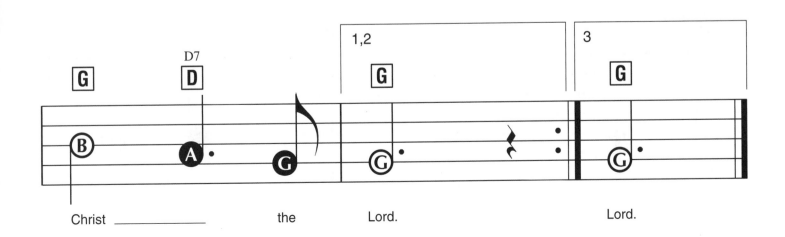

O Come, O Come Immanuel

Registration 3
Rhythm: None

Plainsong, 13th Century
Words translated by John M. Neale
and Henry S. Coffin

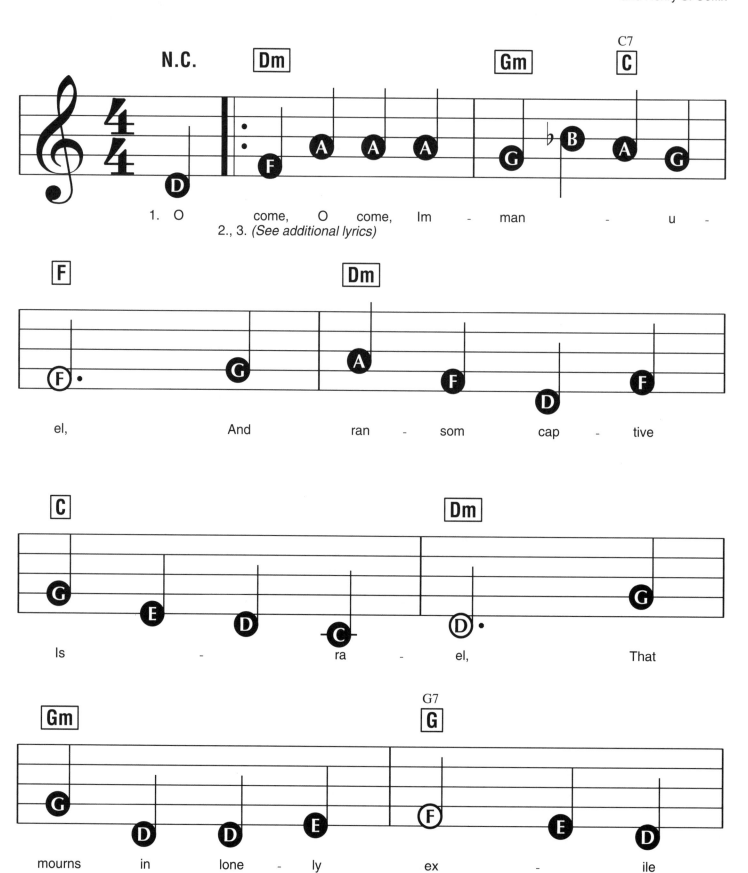

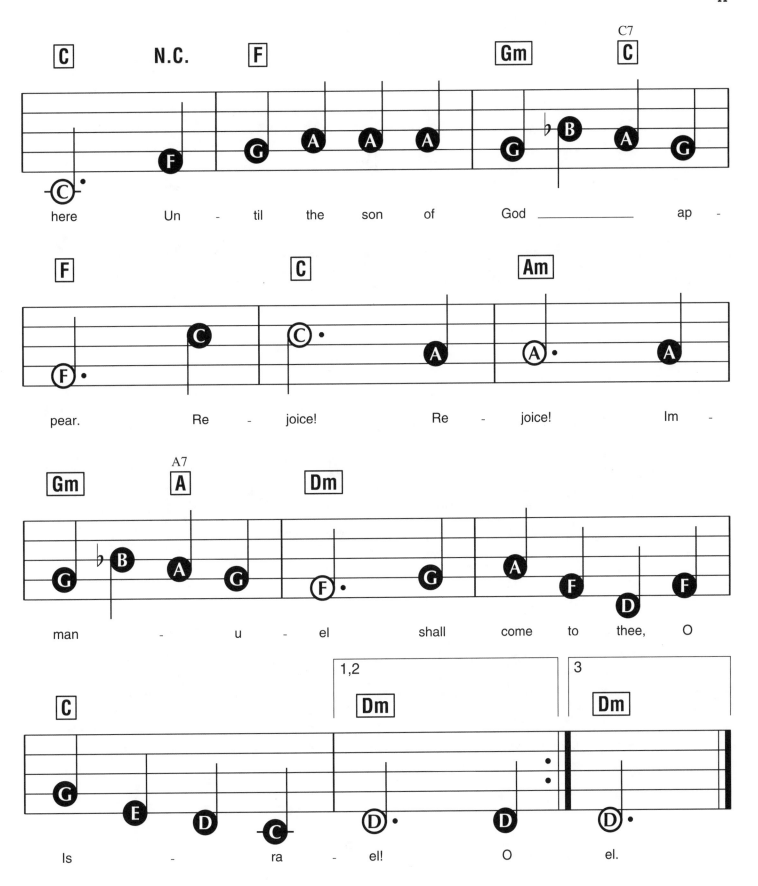

Additional Lyrics

2. O come, Thou Key of David, come,
   And open wide our heav'nly home.
   Make safe the way that leads on high,
   And close the path to misery.

   Rejoice! Rejoice! Immanuel
   Shall come to thee, O Israel.

3. O come, thou Rod of Jesse, free
   Thine own from Satan's tyranny.
   From depths of hell thy people save,
   And give them victory o'er the grave.

   Rejoice! Rejoice! Immanuel
   Shall come to thee, O Israel.

O Holy Night

Registration 6
Rhythm: None

French Words by Placide Cappeau
English Words by John S. Dwight
Music by Adolphe Adam

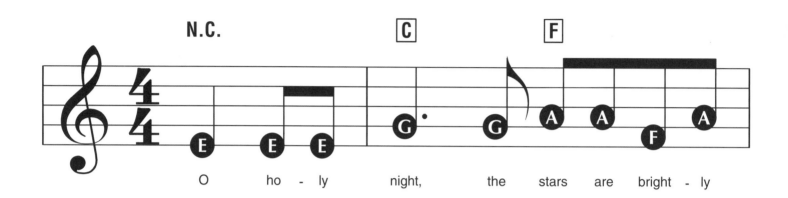

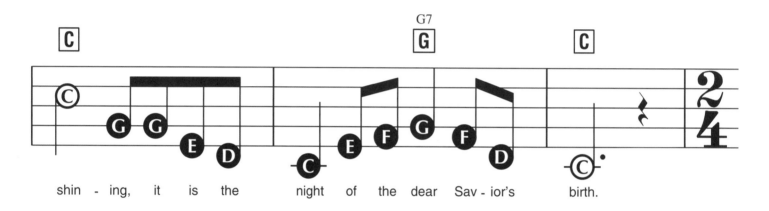

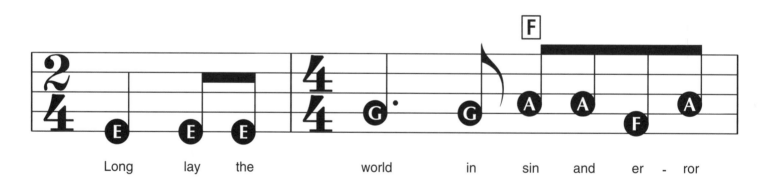

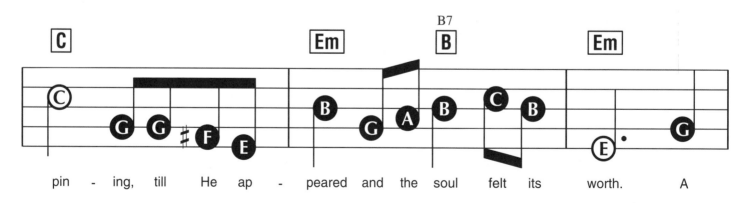

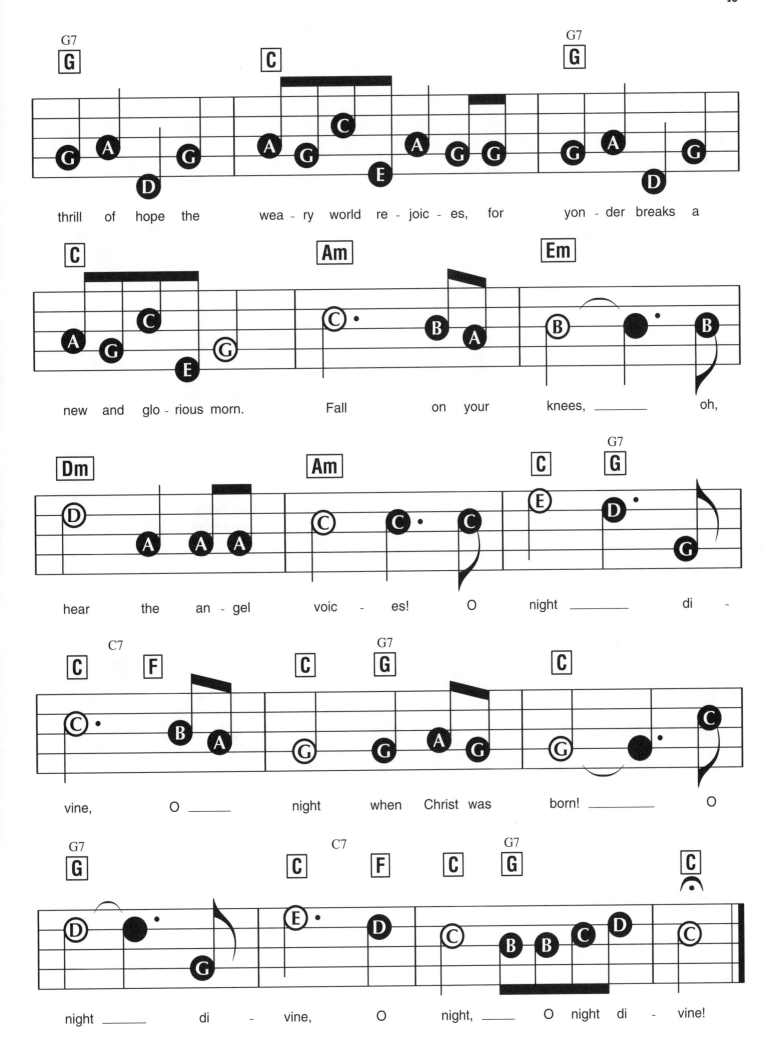

Silent Night

Registration 1
Rhythm: Waltz

Words by Joseph Mohr
Translated by John F. Young
Music by Franz X. Grüber

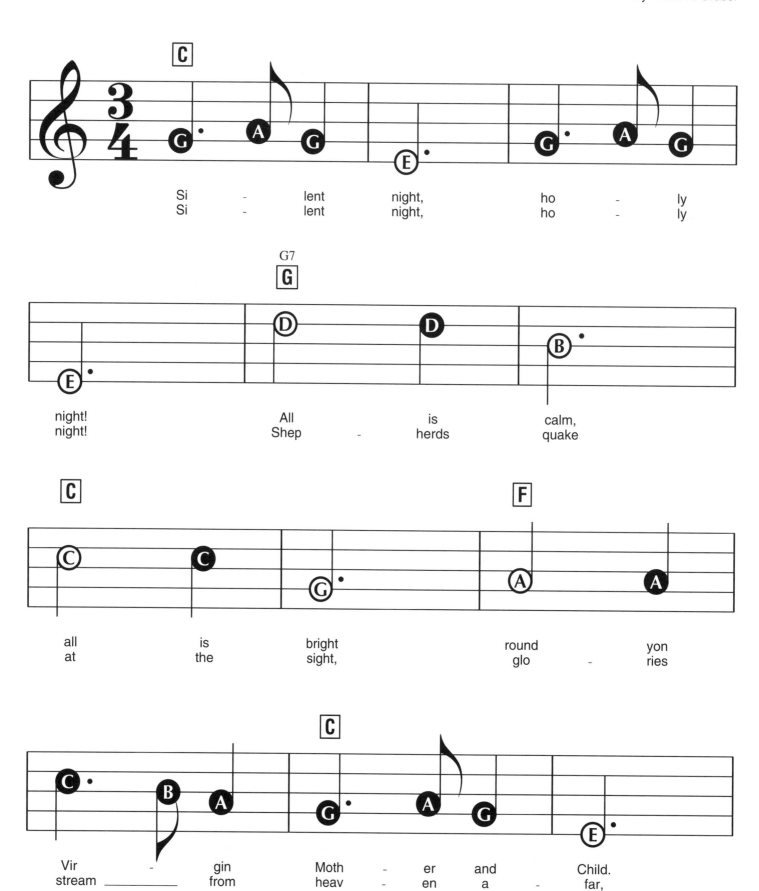

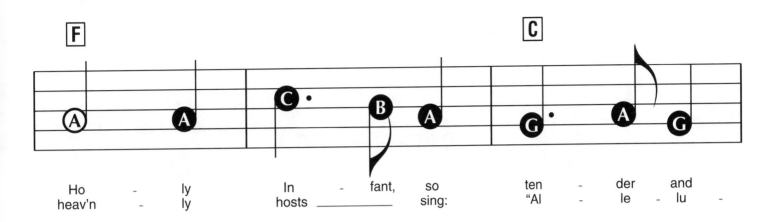

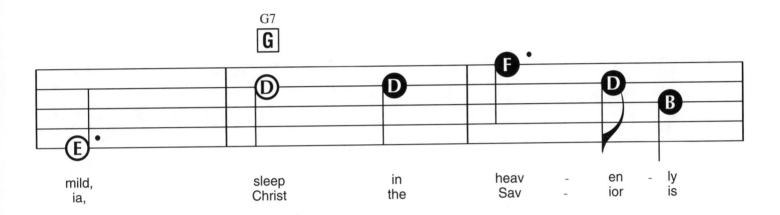

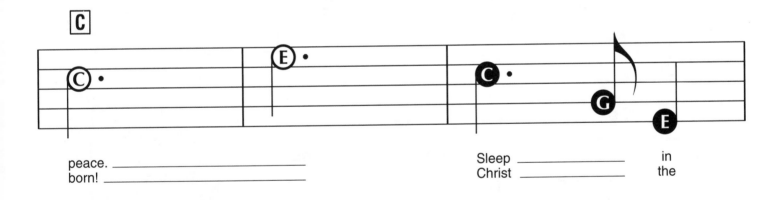

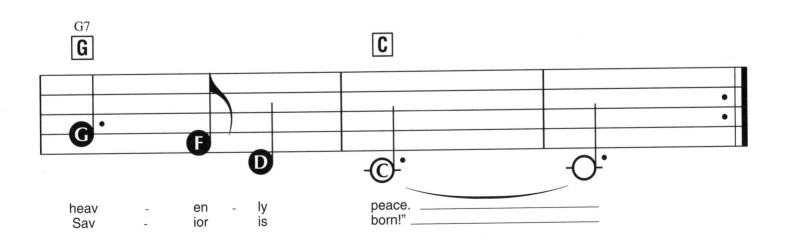

The Twelve Days of Christmas

Registration 5
Rhythm: None

Traditional English Carol

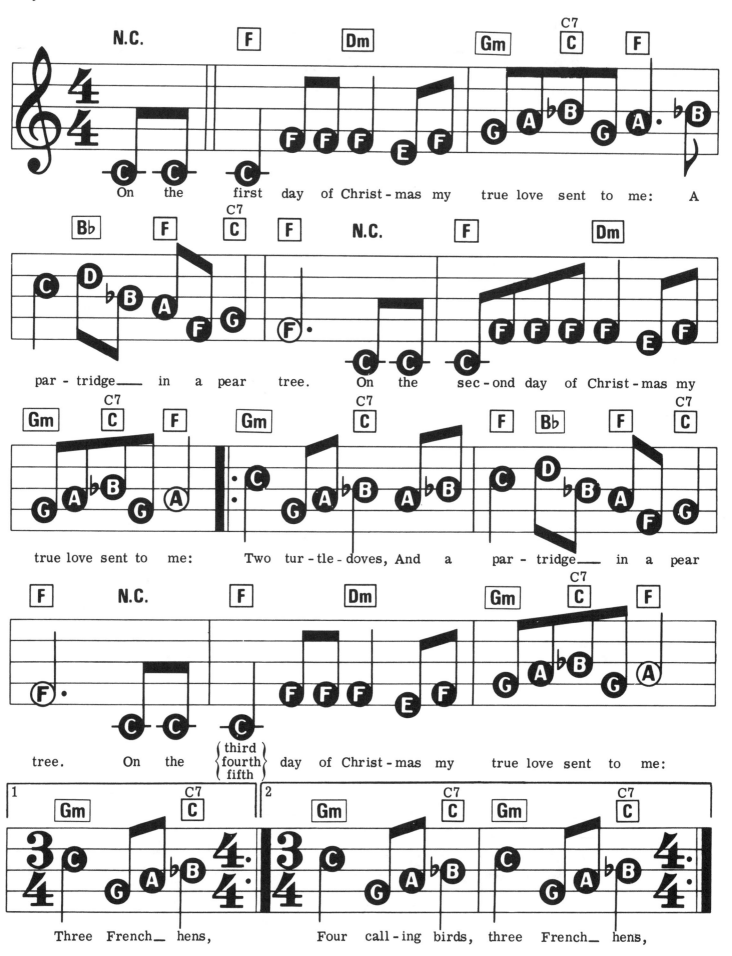

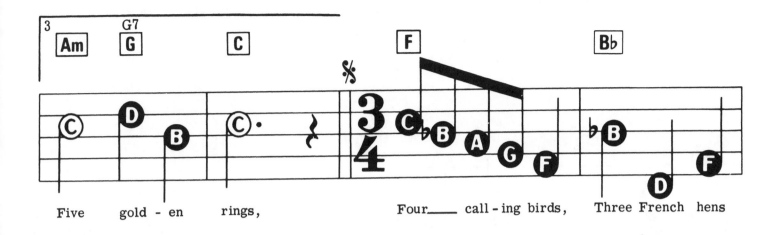

Five gold - en rings, Four____ call - ing birds, Three French hens

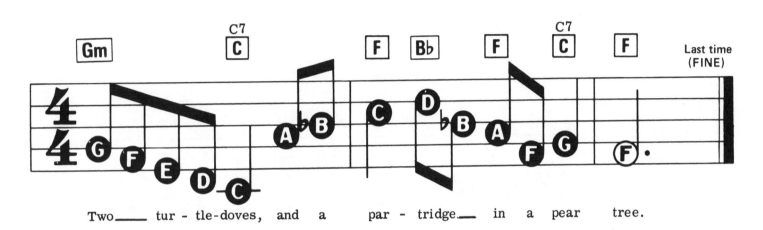

Two____ tur - tle-doves, and a par - tridge___ in a pear tree.

On the {sixth seventh eighth, etc.} day of Christ - mas my true love sent to me_____

D.S. al Fine
(Return to %
Play to Fine)

{
Six geese a - lay - ing
Seven swans a - swim-ming (to 6)
Eight maids a - milk - ing (to 7)
Nine la - dies danc - ing (to 8)
Ten lords a - leap - ing (to 9)
Eleven pi - pers pip - ing (to 10)
Twelve drum-mers drum-ming (to 11)
}

Five gold - en rings.

We Three Kings of Orient Are

Registration 9
Rhythm: Waltz

Words and Music by
John H. Hopkins, Jr.

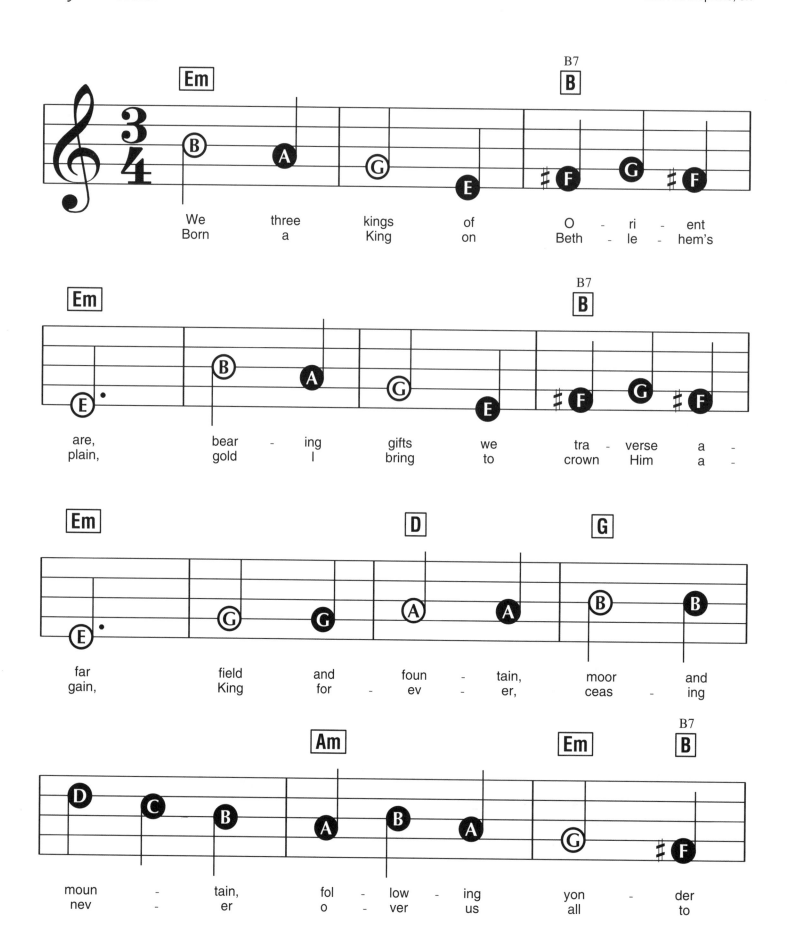

We three kings of O - ri - ent
Born a King on Beth - le - hem's

are, bear - ing gifts we tra - verse a -
plain, gold I bring to crown Him a -

far field and foun - tain, moor and
gain, King for ev - er, ceas - ing

moun - tain, fol - low - ing yon - der
nev - er o - ver us all to

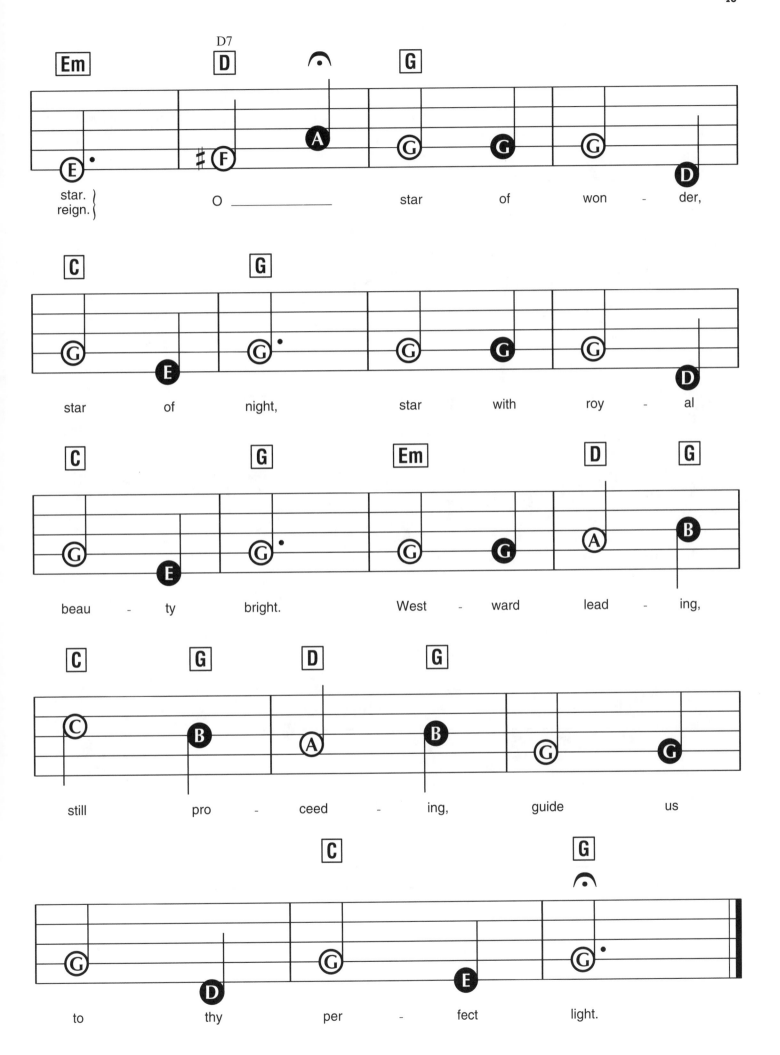

We Wish You a Merry Christmas

Registration 4
Rhythm: None

Traditional English Folksong

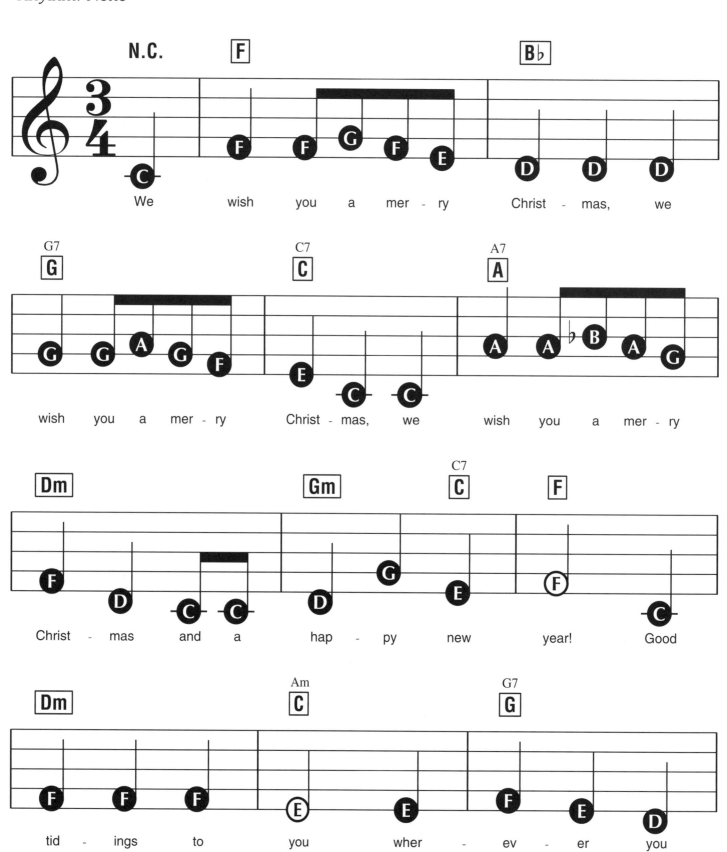

51

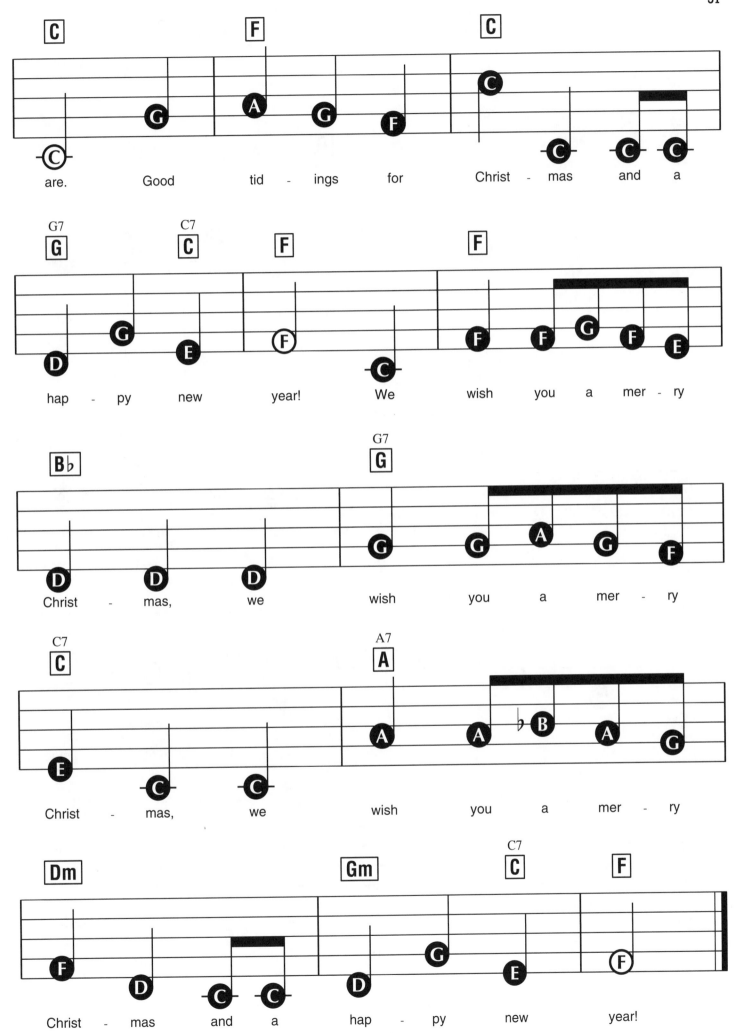

What Child Is This?

Registration 10
Rhythm: Waltz

Words by William C. Dix
16th Century English Melody

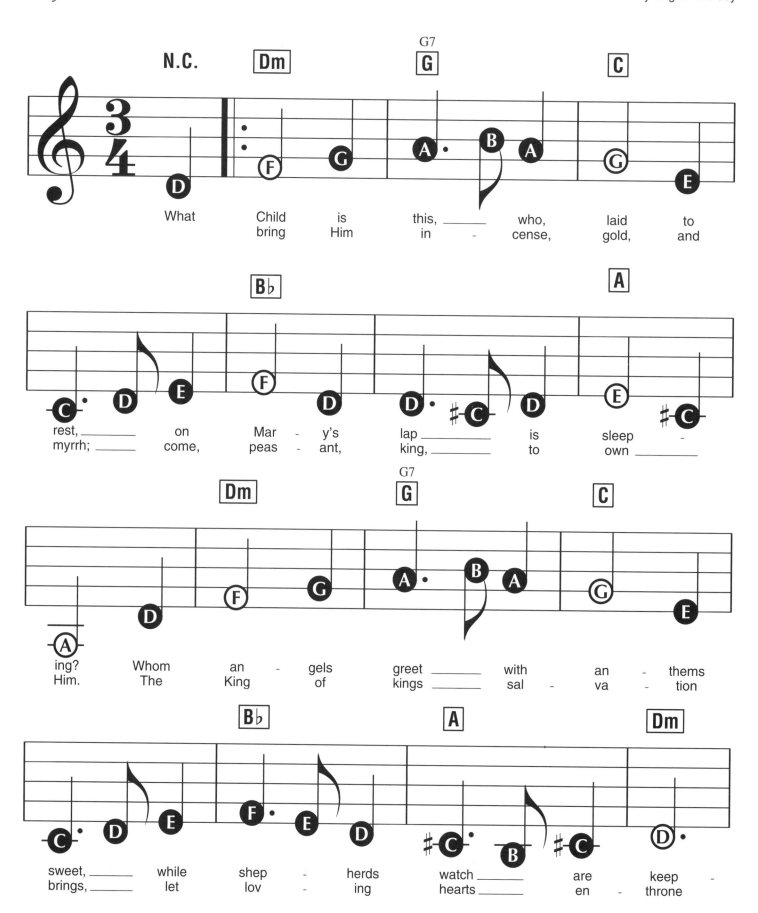

53

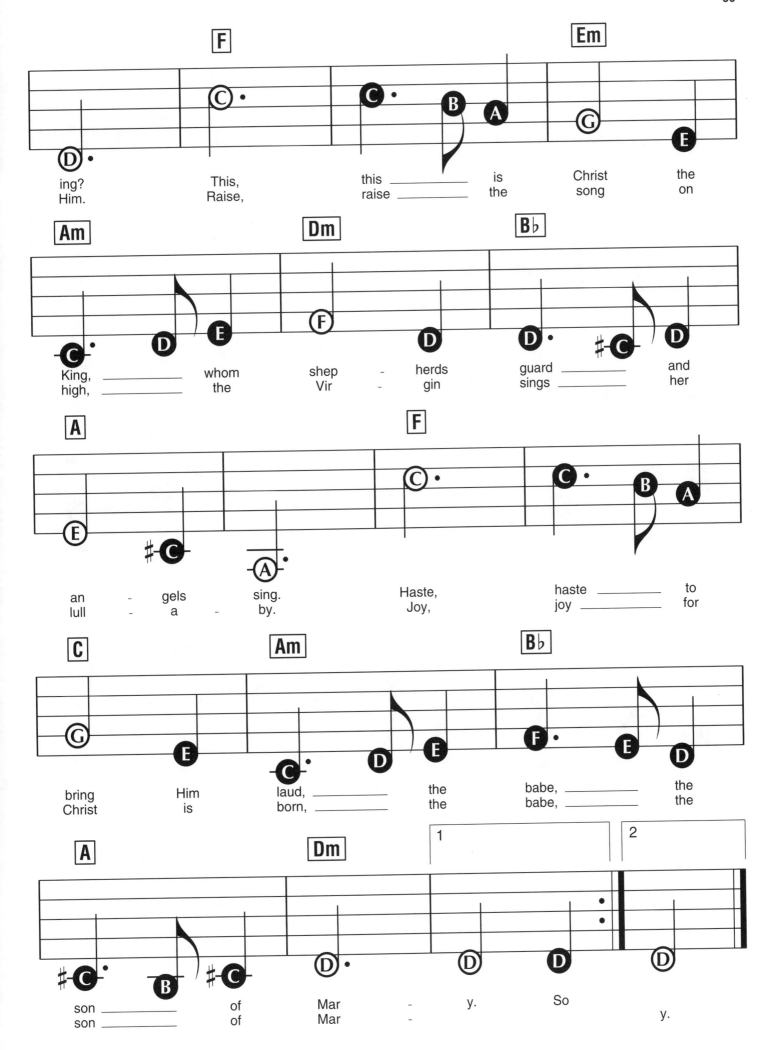

Up on the Housetop

Registration 5
Rhythm: Fox Trot or Swing

Words and Music by
B.R. Handy

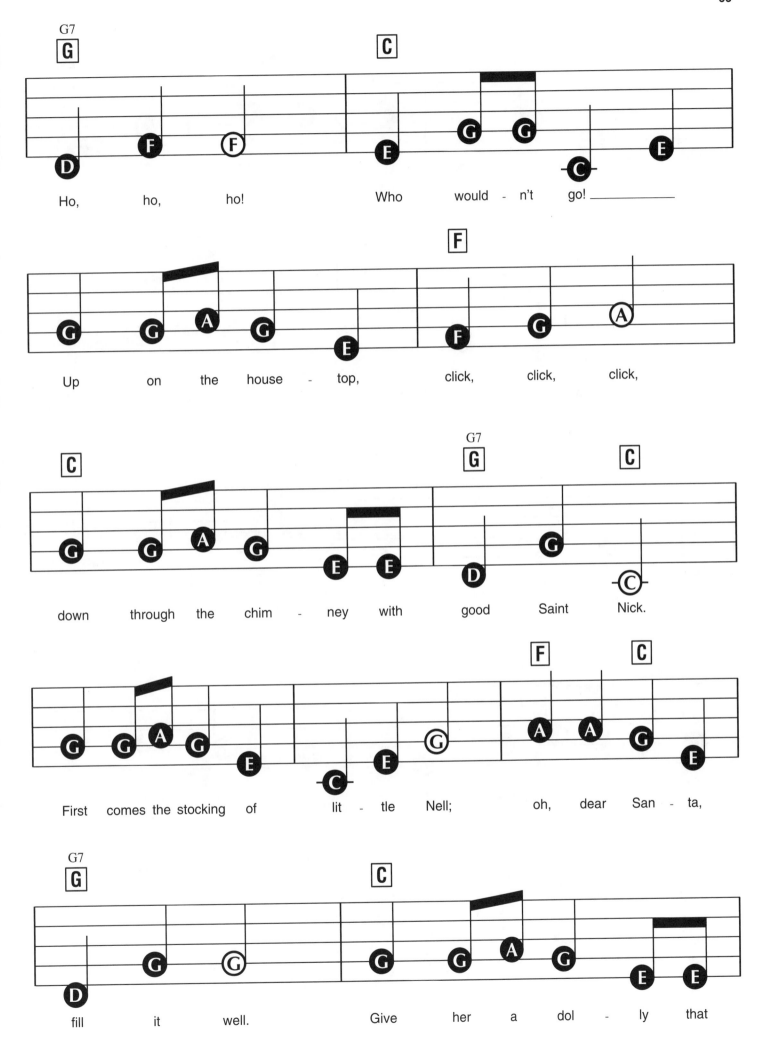

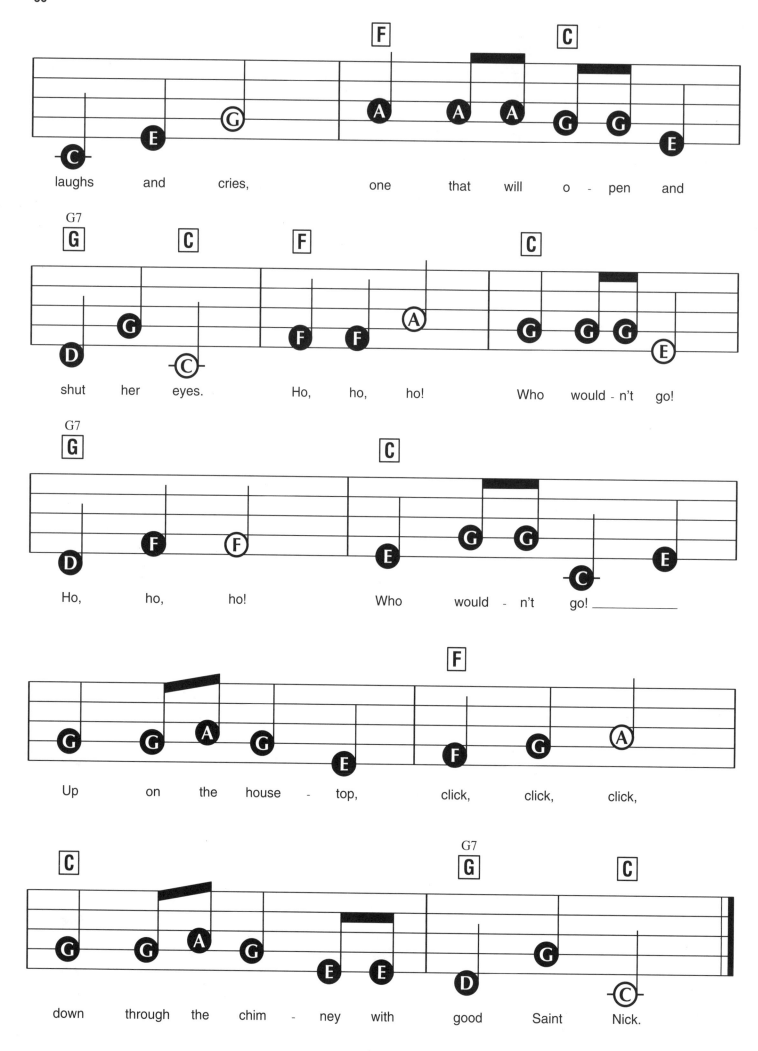